TENNESSEE WI

Sweet Bird of Youth

with commentary and notes by
KATHERINE WEISS

Advisory Editor
MATTHEW ROUDANÉ

METHUEN DRAMA

Methuen Drama Student Edition

10 9 8 7 6 5 4 3 2 1

This edition first published in the United Kingdom in 2010 by Methuen Drama
A & C Black Publishers Limited
36 Soho Square
London W1D 3QY
www.methuendrama.com

By special arrangement with The University of the South, Sewanee,
Tennessee

The proprietor hereby asserts the author's right to be identified as the
author of the works in accordance with the Copyright, Designs and Patents
Act, 1988

Copyright © 1959, 1962, renewed 1987, 1990 by The University of the South

Commentary and notes copyright © Methuen Drama 2010

A CIP catalogue record for this book is available from the British Library

ISBN 978 1 408 11438 4

Playtext typeset by Country Setting, Kingsdown, Kent
Commentary, Notes and Foreword typeset by
SX Composing DTP, Rayleigh, Essex
Printed and bound in Great Britain by
CPI Cox & Wyman, Reading, Berkshire

Contents

Tennessee Williams: 1911–1983   v

Plot   xii

Commentary   xviii
    Context   xviii
    Themes   xx
    Structure, language and style   xxxix
    Characters   xlvi
    Stage, film and television productions   lvii

Further Reading   lx

Foreword   1

SWEET BIRD OF YOUTH   7

Notes   99

Questions for Further Study   105

Tennessee Williams: 1911–83

1908 Williams's sister, Rose Isabelle, is born 19
      November in Columbus, Mississippi.
1911 Thomas Lanier Williams III is born on 26 March in
      Columbus, Mississippi.
1911 Rose, Tom, and their mother, Edwina Dakin Williams,
-18   live with Edwina's parents, the Reverend Walter
      Dakin, an Episcopal priest, and his wife Rosina
      Otte Dakin, chiefly in Clarksdale, while father
      Cornelius Coffin Williams works as a travelling
      salesman.
1918 Williams's younger brother, Walter Dakin, born on
      21 February; the Williams family moves to St Louis
      where father becomes a branch manager at the
      International Shoe Company.
1926 After only one semester at Soldan High School in St
      Louis, Williams transfers to University City High
      School.
1928 Publishes the first story for which he is paid – 'The
      Vengeance of Nitrosis' – in *Weird Tales*. Goes on a
      European trip with his maternal grandfather.
1929 In September, Williams enters the University of
      Missouri and joins Alpha Tau Omega fraternity. In
      October the stock market crashes resulting in the
      Great Depression.
1932 Williams's father withdraws him from the University
      of Missouri for failing ROTC (Reserve Officers
      Training Course) and starts him as a clerk at the
      International Shoe Company, a job he loathes.
1935 First production of Williams's one-act play – *Cairo!
      Shanghai! Bombay!* – by Memphis Garden Players, a
      group of amateur actors.
1936 In January, Williams enrols at Washington

University in St Louis and writes the one-act play
Twenty-Seven Wagons Full of Cotton.

1937   Writes a full-length, leftist play, *Candles to the Sun*,
about a coal-mine strike, staged by the Mummers
(amateur group of actors) in St Louis. Rose is
committed to Farmington (Missouri) State Mental
Hospital; Williams is heartbroken and feels
tremendous guilt.

1937   Studies playwriting at the University of Iowa with
–39   Edward Charles Mabie, nicknamed 'the Boss';
Mummers stage *Fugitive Kind*. Graduates from Iowa
with a BA in English. Writes another leftist play, *Not
About Nightingales*, about a prison riot in
Pennsylvania. Becomes a vagabond, travelling to
New Orleans where he possibly has his first
homosexual experience in the French Quarter.

1939   Meets Audry Wood, his agent for over thirty years.
Signs his name Tennessee Williams for the first time
in a short story 'Field of Blue Children' in *Story
Magazine*. Receives a $100 prize in a competition
organised by the Group Theatre (where Elia
Kazan's wife, Molly Day Thacher, is one of the
readers) for his collection of one-act plays *American
Blues*. Wins a grant of $1,000 from the Rockefeller
Foundation.

1940   Studies playwriting with John Gassner and Erwin
Piscator at the New School for Social Research. His
first professional production of a play – *The Battle of
Angels* – has a disastrous Boston tryout on 30
December but closes on 11 January 1941 after the
City Council protests about its sexual content.

1941   Travels around the country, writing one-act plays,
–42   stories, and poems; visits Key West for the first time;
has the first of his four cataract operations.
Collaborates on *You Touched Me!* with Donald
Windham. Meets Jordan Massee, Sr, a model for
Big Daddy.

1943   Works for Metro-Goldwyn-Mayer (MGM) on a
screenplay *The Gentleman Caller* (later *The Glass*

Menagerie) but is fired after only six months. Rose has a prefrontal lobotomy, leaving her mentally challenged for life; the operation is referenced in *Suddenly Last Summer*.

1944 National Institute for Arts and Letters awards Williams $1,000 for *Battle of Angels*. Margo Jones, theatre founder and longtime friend, directs the one-act play *The Purification* at the Pasadena Playhouse in California. *The Glass Menagerie* premieres in Chicago on 26 December.

1945 *The Glass Menagerie*, Williams's first big success, runs for 561 performances on Broadway, winning the New York Drama Critics' Circle Award and the Donaldson Award. He publishes thirteen one-act plays in *Twenty-Seven Wagons Full of Cotton*.

1947 *A Streetcar Named Desire*, directed by Elia Kazan, opens on 3 December at the Barrymore Theatre on Broadway and runs for 855 performances, spawning two road companies. Williams meets his longtime companion and lover Frank Merlo (1929–63), a US Navy veteran.

1948 Alfred Kinsey's *Sexual Behavior in the Human Male* is
–49 published on 3 January 1948. *Streetcar* wins the triple crown of the Pulitzer, New York Drama Critics' Circle Award and the Donaldson Award. It premieres across the world (e.g. Mexico, Belgium, France, Germany, Sweden). British premiere of *Streetcar* (Sept.) directed by Laurence Olivier, starring wife Vivien Leigh. *One Arm and Other Stories*, a collection of sexually explicit stories, is published. *Summer and Smoke* opens on Broadway.

1950 First (and worst according to Williams) film adaptation of *The Glass Menagerie* released by Warner Brothers. The novel *The Roman Spring of Mrs Stone* is published.

1951 *The Rose Tattoo* opens in New York for 306 performances. Warner Brothers releases film of *Streetcar*, also directed by Kazan and designed by Jo Mielziner; produced by Irene Selznick, former wife of David O. Selznik, producer of *Gone with the Wind*.

1952   *Streetcar* wins National Film Critics' Circle Award. Williams is elected to the National Institute of Arts and Letters. Publishes the story 'Three Players of a Summer Game', the genesis of *Cat on a Hot Tin Roof*.

1953   *Camino Real*, with gay characters and themes, opens on Broadway.

1954   *Hard Candy* (another collection of explicit fiction) is published. Works on drafts of *Cat on a Hot Tin Roof*. Kazan insists on major revisions.

1955   *Cat on a Hot Tin Roof* premieres on 24 March on Broadway and runs for 649 performances, winning Williams his second Pulitzer Prize and third New York Drama Critics' Circle Award; film of *The Rose Tattoo* released; Reverend Walter Dakin dies, aged ninety-seven.

1956   *Baby Doll* screenplay condemned for sexual content by the Catholic Church. *Cat on a Hot Tin Roof* opens in Paris (16 December); it is banned in Ireland. First book of poetry, *In the Winter of Cities*, is published.

1957   *Orpheus Descending* (revision of *Battle of Angels*) closes in New York after 68 performances. Cornelius Coffin Williams dies.

1958   Film version of *Cat on a Hot Tin Roof* is released by MGM, directed and co-written by Richard Brooks; it is Williams's biggest box-office hit; *Suddenly Last Summer* opens Off-Broadway. British premiere of *Cat on a Hot Tin Roof* using Williams's original third act is staged at a private club because of ban by Lord Chamberlain.

1959   *Sweet Bird of Youth*, with antagonist Boss Finley, opens for 375 performances on Broadway. Screen version of *Suddenly Last Summer* is released.

1960   Williams's comedy *Period of Adjustment* opens in New York for 132 performances. Film of *Orpheus Descending*, set in a hellish Delta, opens under the title of *Fugitive Kind*.

1961   Williams's last Broadway success, *The Night of the Iguana*, wins the New York Drama Critics' Circle Award and runs for 316 performances. Film versions of *Summer and Smoke* and *The Roman Spring of Mrs Stone* come out.

1962   The first film version of *Sweet Bird of Youth*, directed by Richard Brooks and starring Paul Newman as Chance Wayne and Geraldine Page as Alexandra Del Lago, opens. *Period of Adjustment* (starring Jane Fonda) is produced

1963   *The Milk Train Doesn't Stop Here Anymore* opens on Broadway. Frank Merlo dies of lung cancer.

1964   Film of *The Night of the Iguana* is released, starring Richard Burton as a drunken clergyman.

1966   *Slapstick Tragedy* (*The Mutilated* and *The Gnadiges Fraulein*) closes after only seven performances.

1967   First version of *The Two-Character Play*, about a brother and sister, opens in London.

1968   *The Seven Descents of Myrtle* (later entitled *Kingdom of Earth*) opens on Broadway for 27 performances; contains graphic sex scene.

1969   *In the Bar of a Tokyo Hotel* premieres 11 May in New York for 23 performances. Williams is committed to psychiatric unit of Barnes Hospital, St Louis, 27–8 June. The Stonewall (named after the gay bar) Riots erupt in New York City, marking the start of the Gay Liberation movement. Williams is baptised a Roman Catholic in Key West.

1970   *Dragon Country: A Book of Plays* is published. Williams appears on the *David Frost Show* and for the first time publicly admits his homosexuality.

1971   *Out Cry* (rewritten version of *The Two-Character Play*) opens on 2 July in Chicago.

1972   *Small Craft Warnings* moves to Broadway for 200 performances; Williams plays the role of Doc, a drunken, disbarred physician – the only time he acts in a professional production of his plays.

1974   *Eight Mortal Ladies: A Book of Stories* is published. *Cat on a Hot Tin Roof* opens at the American Shakespeare Festival Theatre, Stratford, CT, with Williams's final, new third act.

1975 Williams given the Medal of Honor for Literature
      by the National Arts Club. *Memoirs* published, as
      well as a novel, *Moise and the World of Reason*. *Red Devil
      Battery Sign*, occasioned by Watergate, is staged in
      Boston and New York. First Broadway revival of *Cat
      on a Hot Tin Roof* with Williams's final script. The
      Broadway revival of *Sweet Bird of Youth*, starring Irene
      Worth, opens at the Harkness Theatre.

1976 *Eccentricities of a Nightingale* (revision of *Summer and
      Smoke*) premieres in New York.

1977 *Vieux Carré* closes after only 11 performances.
      Second book of poetry, *Androgyne, Mon Amour*,
      published. First televised *Cat on a Hot Tin Roof*.

1978 *A Lovely Sunday for Crève Coeur* opens in New York for
      36 performances.

1979 Receives Presidential Arts Achievement Award.

1980 President Jimmy Carter presents Williams with
      Medal of Freedom. Edwina Dakin Williams dies at
      the age of ninety-five. *Clothes for a Summer Hotel*,
      about Zelda Fitzgerald's madness, opens.

1981 *Something Cloudy, Something Clear* opens Off-Broadway;
      last of Williams's plays to be professionally produced
      while he was alive.

1983 Williams dies on 24 February in New York at the
      Hotel Elysée (Elysian Fields, the 'Land of the Happy
      Dead' in *Streetcar*) after choking on a medicine-bottle
      cap.

1984 Showtime (cable TV) airs *Cat on a Hot Tin Roof*, re-
      shown on PBS TV in 1985.

1985 Tennessee Williams's *Collected Stories* is published.
      Sweet Bird of Youth premières in London.

1988 British revival of *Cat on a Hot Tin Roof*, directed by
      Howard Davies, uses Williams's original script
      (1955), the first production of the play in Britain in
      thirty years.

1990 Davies directs *Cat on a Hot Tin Roof* for its Broadway
      revival.

1994 The London revival of *Sweet Bird of Youth* opens at
      the National Theatre.

1996   Rose Williams dies on 5 September at the age of eighty-eight.

1998   *Not About Nightingales* premieres at London's Royal National Theatre. Written in 1938, the play was rediscovered in the 1980s by Vanessa Redgrave. Corin Redgrave stars as warden Boss Whalen.

2004   Williams Revival at the Kennedy Center.

2005   *Mister Paradise and Other One-Act Plays*, including thirteen previously unpublished one-acts, is released.

2008   Dakin Williams dies on 20 May. *The Traveling Companion and Other Plays* (twelve previously uncollected experimental plays) is published. First professional production of *Cat on a Hot Tin Roof* with a black cast on Broadway (comes to London in 2009).

Plot

Act One

Scene One

Chance Wayne, a twenty-nine-year-old man whose good
looks are fading, has returned to his birthplace, St Cloud,
Florida, with an ageing movie star, Alexandra Del Lago, on
Easter Sunday. While Del Lago sleeps, a coloured waiter,
Fly, delivers a bottle of vodka and Bromo-Seltzer. Fly
recognises Chance as the young man who used to take out
Governor Boss Finley's daughter. Uncomfortable with being
recognised, Chance offers Fly a large tip if he forgets he ever
saw him.

However, word has already got out that Chance has
returned to this Gulf Coast town. After Fly's departure,
George Scudder, St Cloud's local doctor, arrives, trying to
persuade Chance to leave at once. In the process, Scudder
reveals two crucial events that have occurred while Chance
has been away. The first is that Chance's mother has died.
Although he attempted to locate Chance, Chance never
received the letters the doctor sent. The church had to take
up donations to have Mrs Wayne buried. The second event
involves Heavenly Finley, Chance's young love. While
Scudder does not reveal what has happened to Heavenly, he
impresses on Chance that ever since he has become a
'criminal degenerate', he is not welcome in St Cloud. In
fact, the doctor tells Chance that Boss Finley has vowed to
have Chance castrated if he was ever to return to town.
Before leaving, Scudder throws one more bit of devastating
news Chance's way. Scudder and Heavenly will be married
in a month's time.

Stunned, Chance calls Aunt Nonnie, his former ally and
Heavenly's aunt; however, she is unable to speak to him
openly on the phone. At this moment, Del Lago awakens,

bewildered and needing oxygen. From her interaction with Chance, we learn that while fleeing from her failed comeback on screen, travelling incognito as the Princess Kosmonopolis, she picked up Chance at a beach resort in Palm Springs, Florida. He is essentially her gigolo. Yet Chance has not offered to be her driver and male companion merely for money. He has a plan to blackmail her. To execute his plan, he attempts to trick Del Lago into confessing to a federal offence on tape. Along with recalling her failed comeback, she, unknowingly, confides that she smuggled Moroccan hashish into the United States. However, Chance is unable to beat this 'monster'. She calls his bluff, forcing him to go to bed with her if he wants her to sign over her travellers' cheques and stand by a contract, which she drew up in Palm Springs, to introduce Chance into the film industry.

Scene Two

Having obeyed Del Lago, Chance is seen dressing as Del Lago signs her travellers' cheques. As she does this, she persuades Chance to tell her his life story as a screen test of sorts. The rest of the scene consists of Chance recollecting, and perhaps fabricating, a narrative of his past. We learn that Chance first left his birthplace at the age of nineteen. Initially, he appeared to have some success in minor roles in musicals and even appeared on the cover of *Life* magazine. However, as his luck waned, Chance began to prostitute himself before going into the Navy during the Korean War. While in the Navy, Chance suffered from nightmares and began to drink. He tells Del Lago that he hated the routine and discipline required of him in the Navy, and shortly after divulges that he 'cracked up' and was discharged. He returned to St Cloud but noticed a difference in the attitudes of the people who once admired him. For Chance, St Cloud was still a haven because Heavenly, his teenage love, whose nude photo he shows to Del Lago, lives there. Chance reveals, however, that even Heavenly's attitude towards him had changed; the last time he returned to St Cloud, Heavenly urged him to go away, calling him a liar.

After telling his life story to Del Lago, Chance discloses
the later part of his plan. He needs the money and Del
Lago's Cadillac to impress the people of St Cloud, and most
of all Heavenly, convincing them that he is a success.
Moreover, he wants Del Lago to arrange a talent show
celebrating youth and declare Chance and Heavenly the
winners so that they can leave for the West Coast together.

Act Two

Scene One

On the terrace of the Finley home, Boss Finley and George
Scudder discuss how to handle Chance's return, particularly
since Boss Finley will be holding a rally for the Youth for
Tom Finley clubs to state his position on desegregation and
the youth group's violent tactics. This rally will be televised
at the same hotel where Chance and Del Lago are staying.
During this, we learn that Boss Finley's grudge against
Chance stems from the nude photograph of his daughter
which unbeknown to Chance was circulated by the
photographic shop clerk who made extra copies of it. As if
this scandal were not enough, news of Heavenly's operation
to cure her of the venereal disease she contracted from
Chance, which was performed badly by Scudder and left
Heavenly barren, has leaked out. As a result, Boss Finley has
been heckled at previous rallies.

Tom Junior, Finley's violent son and president of the
Youth for Tom Finley clubs, sees Aunt Nonnie run up the
drive. Chance has driven up to the house in Del Lago's
Cadillac and is calling out to Aunt Nonnie. Ignoring him, she
runs to the house. Boss Finley and Tom Junior taunt the old
woman for being gullible and having favoured Chance over
other suitors. After Aunt Nonnie leaves, Tom Junior, when
berated by his father for his promiscuity, confronts his father
with his own promiscuity. Tom Junior informs Boss Finley
that Miss Lucy, Boss's lover, ridicules him by claiming that he
is 'too old for a lover' and has written this insult for all to see
on the mirror of the ladies' room at the hotel. He, we learn, is

not the only person who knows about Boss Finley's promiscuity. Heavenly, who enters reluctantly, scorns her father for his affair. She scolds him for trying to marry her to rich old men rather than allowing her to marry Chance, a boy she loved. Furthermore, she blames her father for Chance's moral decay. In his attempt to compete with these wealthy, ageing men, Chance tried his luck in Hollywood. Boss Finley now bares his plan to silence all rumours of Heavenly's impurity, which are damaging him politically, by having her stand beside him, in white, at the rally.

Scene Two

In the hotel cocktail lounge, an antebellum Southern belle with her index finger bandaged accuses Stuff, the bartender, of breaking her trust by telling others what she had written on the mirror of the ladies' room. Miss Lucy explains that Boss Finley brought her a brooch in an Easter egg. As she opened the velvet box in the egg and went to take out the diamond pin, Boss Finley shut the lid on her finger. Noticing a stranger in the bar and suspecting that he is the heckler, Miss Lucy seeks out revenge on her former lover. She promises to aid the Heckler, giving him a jacket and tie so that he will be able to enter the ballroom where the televised rally will take place.

Chance enters, but shortly after getting his martini, is called out to the royal grove and beach by Aunt Nonnie who wishes to speak to him. She urges Chance to leave town and stop dreaming of a future that will not come true. Taking a pill and washing it down with a drink, Chance reminisces over his stage debut and the loss of his virginity. Aunt Nonnie reminds Chance that rather than winning first or second place, as he says he did, he only received an honourable mention. Although Aunt Nonnie has tender memories of Chance, she is no longer charmed by him; she tells him that his real flaw is that he cannot confront his failures.

Once alone, Chance takes another pill. A small group Chance once socialised with spot him. The ladies in the group leave while their husbands, Scotty and Bud, remain.

Taking advantage of his weakness, Scotty and Bud heckle
Chance. Perhaps as a threat, Bud tells Chance of the
emasculation of a black man – a fate that Chance will face if
he remains in St Cloud. Insightfully, Chance condemns the
racist act, calling castration a crime of 'sex-envy'. He also
doubts that Heavenly will accompany her father in such a
despicable rally.

Miss Lucy, attempting to ease the tension between
Chance, Bud and Scotty, reveals that Dan Hatcher, the
assistant manager of the hotel, saw Chance working in Palm
Beach as a beach boy. Perhaps Chance's only friend in St
Cloud, Miss Lucy, afraid of what will happen to Chance if
he stays, offers to drive Chance to the airport. He turns her
offer down.

Del Lago enters, dishevelled and high. She has had an
epiphany. Chance's return to St Cloud has made her feel
something tender for him and she wants him to help her be
good and kind. Although Chance has no desire to leave with
Del Lago, when he sees Tom Junior and Scotty, he is
affectionate and kind to the ageing star, but only to save
himself from imminent harm. Boss Finley enters, sees
Chance, raises his cane and nearly strikes him before letting
it drop. Stunned, Chance watches Heavenly go to the
platform with her vicious father. All this, the Heckler
witnesses.

Still by Chance's side, Del Lago is silenced by fear when
Hatcher, Bud, Scotty and Tom Junior approach. She senses
danger as the men try to convince Chance to step outside.
He refuses, but in the course of this Tom Junior reveals that
Chance polluted his sister with a venereal disease which he
contracted from one of the many women who paid his way.
Again, Del Lago tries to convince Chance to flee – the only
action to take, she claims, after failure is flight. He does not,
however, listen to her. Instead, he calls for a wheelchair to
have her taken away. Miss Lucy and Stuff turn on the
television to watch the rally. The back wall of the stage
projects the image of Boss Finley, speaking and being
humiliated by the Heckler who is dragged out and beaten.
Heavenly is escorted out, weeping.

Act Three

Past midnight in the hotel room, Del Lago speaks to the operator trying to find a driver so that she can flee St Cloud. The rally has degenerated into a riot. Chance is seen briefly by the audience; as he hears others, he ducks into the shadows. Looking for Chance, Hatcher, Tom Junior, Bud and Scotty force their way into the hotel room and threaten Alexandra Del Lago with violence if she does not leave.

After they have left, Chance, who is shaken, makes his way to the room. There, he commits one more desperate act. He phones Sally Powers, a journalist and friend of Del Lago's, and attempts to have Del Lago praise him and Heavenly as new talent. However, Chance fails again. Del Lago learns that her comeback was not a failure and, caught up by the news, keeps Chance away from the phone; she does not mention him. After the phone call, they struggle, trying to get one another to look in the mirror. Del Lago taunts Chance with his ageing, his lack of achievement in contrast to her and his crime towards Heavenly. He moves to strike her but instead punches himself in the stomach.

Following this struggle, a change occurs in Del Lago. She is fearful, lonely and tender, knowing that her comeback will not last and that time will destroy her eventually. Out of pity for herself and Chance, she again asks him to join her. He refuses in recognition of his doom and, once Del Lago departs, Chance with a 'sort of deathbed dignity' (96) waits for Tom Junior and the other thugs to castrate him.

Commentary

Context

Sweet Bird of Youth comes from the middle period of Tennessee Williams's career. Williams met with great success in the 1940s to mid-1950s with *The Glass Menagerie* (1944), *A Streetcar Named Desire* (1947) and *Cat on a Hot Tin Roof* (1955). After his first two successes, Williams began writing 'a varied assortment of one-act plays and sketches', which, according to Drewey Wayne Gunn, would eventually become *Sweet Bird of Youth*. He points out that 'about 450 pages of manuscripts . . . remain from this incubatory stage' (Gunn, 26–7). Moreover, with *Sweet Bird of Youth*, Williams 'began a new process of trying out a "work in progress" in a regional or off-Broadway theatre, revising it heavily both during rehearsals and after he had had the benefit of a full production' (Murphy, 135).

In 1957, Williams's success was met with the disappointing reception of *Orpheus Descending* which opened in New York City in March. In May, his father died. Although his father was a source of pain and sorrow for Williams because he taunted his son for not being interested in sports and did not understand his desire to write, the failure of *Orpheus Descending* and of the death of Cornelius Coffin Williams led to feelings of depression. Shortly after the death of his father, Williams began to see a psychoanalyst.

The following two years proved to be much more productive. With the opening of the *Garden District*, comprising *Suddenly Last Summer* and *Something Unspoken*, the London premiere of *Cat on a Hot Tin Roof* and other theatre activity in 1958, Williams stopped going to psychoanalysis and travelled to Europe in June. Once back in America, Williams and Elia Kazan began preparing for the Broadway debut of *Sweet Bird of Youth*. Elia Kazan, who had attended the try-outs in Coral Gables, Florida, directed the play and aided Williams in his revisions.

Williams's work has been compared both to his contemporaries and to playwrights of the past. Philip C. Kolin draws a link between Williams and Eugene O'Neill, claiming that O'Neill's *Desire Under the Elms* 'is something of a palimpsest in the Williams canon' (23). In Williams's *A Streetcar Named Desire*, *Kingdom of the Earth* and *Sweet Bird of Youth*, O'Neill's play can be found in similarities in plot, setting and in the biblical allusions. Kolin goes on to show that the character of Boss Finley may have stemmed from O'Neill's play. Ephraim Cabot, O'Neill's tyrannical Puritan farmer, bears a striking resemblance to Williams's Boss Finley, as both struggle to maintain their power.

In addition to drawing on O'Neill's theatrical genius, Williams learned a great deal from William Faulkner, a novelist of the Southern Gothic tradition (see p. xlvi). Faulkner's novel of 1940, *The Hamlet*, which was made into the award-winning film *The Long, Hot Summer*, bears striking similarities to *Sweet Bird of Youth*. Boss Finley, for instance, may be based in part on Will Varner, the domineering father and corrupt businessman, who owns most of the small Mississippi town. Moreover, like Chance Wayne whose presence threatens the political stability of St Cloud, Ben Quick, an outsider trying to make a name for himself, threatens the stability of Varner's quiet Mississippi town and home because of his dangerous reputation as a barn burner. Interestingly, Martin Ritt's film of 1958 and Williams's play both starred Paul Newman as the outsider attempting to rise above his lower socio-economic background.

While in O'Neill and Faulkner Williams may have found his literary fathers, in William Inge, author of *Come Back, Little Sheba* (1950) and *Picnic* (1953), he found a kindred spirit. His close friendship and brief love affair with the playwright Inge had an impact on *Sweet Bird of Youth*. Ralph F. Voss shows that Williams's and Inge's careers in the world of theatre were similar in many ways. Both authors had won Pulitzer prizes, both worked with the director Elia Kazan and both wrote about sexuality in daring new ways. Williams and Inge often spoke about their work and read each other's plays, and thus ultimately influenced each other.

Other playwrights sharing the stage with Williams were Arthur Miller and Edward Albee, both of whom admired Williams. After seeing *A Streetcar Named Desire*, Miller 'was inspired to work even more precisely with his language in a play he was struggling with at the time' (Roudané, 2–3); this play would later turn into Miller's masterpiece *Death of a Salesman* (1949). As well as being drawn to the poetic language of Williams's plays, Miller shared with Williams a distrust of the so-called American Dream – a dream that was thinly disguised consumer capitalism. In addition to a critique of the American Dream, a theme that Albee in *The Zoo Story* (1959) and *Who's Afraid of Virginia Woolf?* (1962) also took up, these playwrights 'produced new and radical theater that challenged and undermined the Cold War order' (Savran, ix). All three playwrights worked to upset the political climate of the 1950s and 1960s, and Miller and Albee learned from Williams, who had been pushing the limits of theatre since 1944. By challenging the nuclear family, masculinity and sexuality, Williams, Miller and Albee attempted to dismantle the patriarchal, anti-communist sentiments and politics of 1950s and 1960s America.

Themes

'The Catastrophe of Success' and Sweet Bird of Youth
After the success of *The Glass Menagerie* and just days before he was to see his second Broadway play open, Williams wrote a bitter critique of success and the Hollywood Dream. This essay, 'The Catastrophe of Success', first appeared in the *New York Times* on 30 November 1947. Though he would go on to write *Sweet Bird of Youth* among several other successful plays, the importance of this essay is felt throughout his body of work and is crucial to understanding the themes of lost youth and broken dreams in *Sweet Bird of*

Youth. In the essay, Williams begins to define his experience as 'not unique. Success has often come that abruptly into the lives of Americans. The Cinderella story is our favourite national myth, the cornerstone of the film industry if not of the Democracy itself' (*Glass Menagerie*, 99). By evoking the Cinderella story, Williams does more than argue that in America it was possible to move suddenly from rags to riches. He brings an awareness of class divisions when he claims that 'Hotel service is embarrassing [. . .] Nobody,' he writes, 'should have to clean up anybody else's mess in this world' (102). Williams's characters are plagued with the embarrassment that comes with belonging to the lower socio-economic classes – the classes that clean up after the rich. *Sweet Bird of Youth*'s protagonist Chance Wayne, we discover in Act Two, was once a bartender at the Royal Palms Hotel where he has returned with Alexandra Del Lago, an ageing movie star. Like so many of Williams's protagonists, Chance is in a desperate struggle to become 'Cinderella' and tries to attain his ambition through the film industry. Yet while the Cinderella story is a feasible dream (success does come abruptly to some who seek their names to appear on the Silver Screen), it is not easy to achieve as we see in his desperate struggle to be 'somebody'.

In the 'Catastrophe of Success', Williams recognises, too, that the 'happily ever after' in the Cinderella story is nothing but a myth. For those who achieve fame and wealth, the very problem of their success, a problem that Alexandra Del Lago and Boss Finley face, is that of identity:

> the public Somebody you are when you 'have a name' is a fiction created with mirrors and that the only somebody worth being is the solitary and unseen you that existed from your first breath and which is the sum of your actions and so is constantly in a state of becoming under your own volition – and knowing these things, you can even survive the catastrophe of Success! (104)

The identities both Del Lago and Boss Finley create to hold on to their public are familiar to most American audiences; they are clichés still present in American media – whether it

is in the political arena or the Hollywood scene. Boss Finley
has made a name for himself by evoking the rags-to-riches
myth – the political leader who rose from poverty to lead
the common man into better days. On the television screen
broadcasting his speech nationwide, the old stag boasts, 'I
got a mission that I hold sacred to perform in the
Southland. When I was fifteen I came down barefooted out
of the red clay hills. Why? Because the Voice of God called
me to execute this mission' (84). Although Boss Finley may
have been a common hillbilly, he has turned into a
'monster', a corrupt political figure who has filled his
pockets with oil money and allowed innocent black men to
suffer racially motivated crimes. Likewise, Alexandra Del
Lago has invented herself. When Chance reveals his life
story to Del Lago in Act One, Scene Two, the Princess
interrupts with 'BEAUTY! Say it! Say it! What you had was
beauty! I had it! I say it, with pride, no matter how sad,
being gone, now' (35). In this and in her sometimes coarse
expressions, she reveals that, unlike her pseudonym, she has
risen from rags as well. In other words, Del Lago, like
Chance and Boss Finley, comes from humble beginnings. In
her flight, she has created yet another self, the Princess
Kosmonopolis – a name that reveals that this royal diva is in
exile. Chance, wanting badly to become famous and
continually failing to do so, also has a fictional identity,
apparent in his drastic shifts from fragile and lost to a false
confidence.

Although Del Lago and Boss Finley have negotiated their
fictional identities with that of their private selves, the
mirrors have begun to show the downfall of their public
selves. When telling Chance about her 'tragic' comeback in
Act One, Scene One, Del Lago reveals:

> The glorious comeback, when I turned fool and came back …
> The screen's a very clear mirror. There's a thing called a
> close-up. The camera advances and you stand still and your
> head, your face, is caught in the frame of the picture with a
> light blazing on it and all your terrible history screams while
> you smile. (25)

Del Lago explains that after she heard the audience gasp at the close-up she fled the auditorium and kept on running in a desperate flight from the public. The camera has awoken her to the ticking of the clock that whispers 'Loss, loss, loss' (*Glass Menagerie*, 105).

In *Sweet Bird of Youth* Williams again uses the mirror to create tension between characters. Tom Junior confronts his father, Boss Finley, with the fact that Miss Lucy, the Boss's mistress, has used her lipstick to write 'Boss Finley [. . .] is too old to cut the mustard' (50) on the mirror of the hotel's ladies' room. In other words, she exposes his lack of sexual virility and by extension his lack of political potency – she shatters the fiction he has been struggling to keep up.

In the final battle between Chance and the Princess, the mirror is used a last time. After Del Lago's phone conversation with Sally Powers, a conversation that has informed Del Lago that her comeback was a success after all, Chance, infuriated that Del Lago has not mentioned his own talent, forcibly turns her to the mirror: 'Look in that mirror. What do you see in that mirror?'

> **Princess**   I see – Alexandra Del Lago, artist and star!
> Now it's your turn, you look and what do you see?
> **Chance**   I see – Chance Wayne . . .
> **Princess**   The face of a Franz Albertzart, a face that
> tomorrow's sun will touch without mercy. Of course, you
> were crowned with laurel in the beginning, your gold hair was
> wreathed with laurel, but the gold is thinning and the laurel
> has withered. Face it – pitiful monster. (95)

Chance's inability to fill in who he is when looking in the mirror suggests that he recognises his failure to become a star and artist like Del Lago. He is not even able to convince himself that he will be one. After he falters to define himself as anyone other than a man whose chances are all spent, Del Lago parallels Chance to Franz Albertzart, a young man who, failing to make it in the movies, is fated to be the male companion of an elderly lady. Chance, like Albertzart, has two choices: to be Del Lago's gigolo (a form of castration) or to face Tom Finley and his gang of thugs.

Ultimately, like the abruptness of success the fall from that success can be just as sudden.

Despite his critique of success, failure was even bitterer for Williams. In 1957, *Orpheus Descending* met with disappointing reviews and audience turn-out. The show closed only two months after it had opened on Broadway. *Sweet Bird of Youth*, although written in 1952 and receiving its try-outs in 1956, was first produced on Broadway two years after the dismal reception of *Orpheus Descending*. Despite some of the criticism the play received, particularly of its potentially confusing plot development, *Sweet Bird of Youth* was well-received by audiences and is now held in high regard among scholars and theatre buffs for its experimentation with 'plastic theatre' and Williams's even bolder attempts to stage subject matter that was deemed too sensitive for modern audiences.

Preaching hate
Tennessee Williams's concern with humanity's violence and cruelty and his ponderings about the causes of such savagery are evident in both *Sweet Bird of Youth* and his contemplations on the play. In his 'Foreword' to the play, he reveals that during the time he struggled to write *Sweet Bird of Youth* he was full of anger and envy, much like his character Chance Wayne. He wrote to a friend at this time that 'We are all civilised people, which means that we are all savages at heart but observing a few amenities of civilised behavior'. Human existence, then, for Williams, was a thinly veiled savagery, a condition that Williams had not risen above. According to Williams, we are all susceptible to releasing our savagery. Williams sets out to expose 'a good many human weaknesses and brutalities' in his plays (*Where I Live*, 109), and openly admits that he, too, embodies such weaknesses. These human failings, his scenario for the play further reveals, are the 'betrayal of people's hearts by personal and social corruption, identifying the sources of corruption as the individual will-to-power and the fierce competition in capitalist society' (Murphy, 136). The

individual will-to-power, that disease that Chance is infected
with, the disease Williams maps out in 'The Catastrophe of
Success', is of course the desire for fame and fortune. The
identification of capitalism, which is linked to the individual
will-to-power, as being one of the other corrupting forces is
crucial to understanding Williams's play. Like his
contemporaries, Arthur Miller and William Inge, Williams
is highly critical of 1940s and 1950s America – an America
saturated with an ideology of individualism and capitalism,
but an ideology that does not allow all Americans equal
footing in the competition.

Written in 1952 but revised several times until its Broadway
debut in 1959, *Sweet Bird of Youth* resonates with the troubled
climate of the Eisenhower era (1952–60), McCarthyism
(1947–57) and racial tension in the South – a time when
communists, homosexuals and people of colour were not
tolerated within mainstream America. As a Southern, gay
writer, that is, an outsider in an America that was desperately
trying to hold on to a unified white, heterosexual identity,
Williams was conscious of the troubled times this play depicts.
In his 'Foreword' to *Sweet Bird of Youth*, Williams, keenly aware
of the intolerance for those who challenged white America by
being left-wing, non-heterosexual, or non-white, stated
profoundly, 'I think that hate is a thing, a feeling, that can only
exist where there is no understanding'. As an example, Boss
Finley is one of the few of Williams's characters that neither he
nor the audience has sympathy for. Boss Finley and his son,
Tom Junior, have no understanding of the changing world.
They do, however, understand how to use rhetoric to
perpetuate their race crimes.

The Eisenhower era is sometimes romanticised as a time
of prosperity and consumerism. Nearly everyone was said to
have a television, a car and a washing machine – luxuries
which previously were not commonplace items in the
average middle-class household. However, this period was
also wrought with fear and hate. The Republican Senator
Joe McCarthy, who won the respect of both President
Dwight Eisenhower and President Harry Truman before
him, succeeded in stirring up hate and fear in his attempt to

rid America of political dissidents. The House on Un-American Activities (HUAC) was formed in 1938, but McCarthy did not lead his anti-Red campaign until the early 1950s at which time the hearings were also televised. Among those who were questioned and silenced were playwrights, directors and actors. Elia Kazan, who directed the debut of *Sweet Bird of Youth*, was one such individual. If the committee found that the individual on trial was guilty, he/she was blacklisted from the industry. As a consequence, many in theatre and Hollywood found themselves out of work. Fear soon spread throughout the American entertainment business. In fact, these hearings had such a detrimental effect on theatre and film that one New York theatre critic, Brook Atkinson, was moved to blame McCarthyism for the lousy Broadway season in 1952.[1]

This play is deeply rooted in an era of racial segregation. The Civil Rights Act of America was not passed by Congress until 1964, five years after this play premiered on Broadway and twelve years after the play was initially conceived. Williams's childhood and much of his adult life (he was forty-one years of age when he wrote *Sweet Bird of Youth*) was spent witnessing legally sanctioned racist policies and racist acts. Along with the legally sanctioned segregation, it was not uncommon between the years of 1882 to 1968 (though occurrences became increasingly rare after 1964) for black men to be lynched by white mobs. Many of the lynchings, which sometimes involved castration, were acts of retribution; white populations took it on themselves to 'punish' black men for 'raping' white women, a violation of the Jim Crow laws (1887–1965) which made it illegal for black men to have *any* sexual relations with white women. While the accusations of 'rape' were often made when such violence took place, many black men were mutilated without evidence.[2]

[1] Richard H. Rovere, *Senator Joe McCarthy*, Berkeley and Los Angeles, University of California Press, 1996, p. 9.
[2] David Pilgrim, 'What Was Jim Crow?', Museum of Racist Memorabilia, Ferris State University, 2000 (www.ferris.edn/jimcrow).

Indeed, the fear of miscegenation is crucial to the play's political climate. While the cast is predominately white and Southern, Chance's fate is paralleled to a black man who is castrated by the Youth for Tom Finley gang to send the message that they will not allow black men to taint the purity of white women. Boss Finley makes clear his position on the desegregation debate. Speaking to his daughter, Heavenly, he explains:

> I'm relying a great deal on this campaign to bring in young voters for the crusade I'm leading. I'm all that stands between the South and the black days of Reconstruction. And you and Tom Junior are going to stand there beside me in the grand crystal ballroom, as shining examples of white Southern youth – in danger. (56)

Boss Finley repeats this racist rhetoric during his television appearance. While Chance and Miss Lucy watch and comment on the speech, the audience hears the ageing politician bark his racist propaganda:

> As you all know I had no part in a certain operation on a young black gentleman. I call that incident a deplorable thing.
> . . .] However . . . I understand the emotions that lay behind it. The passion to protect by this violent emotion something that we hold sacred: our purity of our own blood! (85)

In the early sketches for the play, Boss Finely was drawn from the real life political leader Huey Long, who served as Louisiana's governor from 1928 to 1932 and US Senator from 1932 to 1935. This right-wing politician's views on miscegenation left much to be desired (Parker, par. 1). While Elia Kazan is credited with softening the character perhaps because of Kazan's own guilt for naming names when questioned by the HUAC, Boss Finley remains a problematic character. He is 'neither Kazan's "sincere" statesman and caring father, nor the hateful political and domestic bully that Williams had come to consider him' (Parker, par. 18). Disliked by readers and audience but not despised by them, Boss Finley's wrath against Chance is in part understandable; after all, Chance did infect the lovely Heavenly with a sexually transmitted disease.

Part of the problem with the character of Boss Finley is
that it is unclear whether he believes that black men are a
physical threat to white womanhood or whether he uses the
rhetoric of the fear of blood contamination to further his
political career and protect his oil money. He does, after all,
attempt to marry his daughter to oil tycoons. Heavenly
confronts her father with his greedy intentions: 'you took me
out of St Cloud, and tried to force me to marry a fifty-year-
old money bag that you wanted something out of –' (53).
Perhaps afraid that Chance would corrupt more than
Heavenly's body – that is, that he would ruin her social
status and thus his own status – Boss Finley employs this
rhetoric in his hatred of Chance. Williams complicates the
matter in that Chance has polluted Heavenly's body.
Repeatedly, the disease that Heavenly contracted from
Chance is referred to as 'rot' (95, 97) and something only
'whores' (45, 81) contract. Having infected Heavenly with a
venereal disease which results in a badly performed
hysterectomy, he will face the knife at the end of the play.

Although we understand the anger of Boss Finley and
Tom Junior, their retribution does not fit the crime.
Williams is able to ridicule the Boss Finleys who 'preach
hate' (79–80) and see desegregation and ruptures in the class
system (Chance is of a lower economic social group) as a
danger to white women's sexual purity in the South.

The Korean War
Having made love to Alexandra Del Lago in Act One,
Scene Two, Chance tells the Princess his life story. While
much of his story appears to be exaggerated boasting
(beginning with his being a twelve-pound baby), Chance's
account of his stint in the Navy appears to be genuine. He
recalls:

> when I came home for those visits, man oh man how that
> town buzzed with excitement. I'm telling you, it would blaze
> with it, and then that thing in Korea came along. I was about
> to be sucked into the Army so I went into the Navy, because a

sailor's uniform suited me better, the uniform was all that
suited me, though. (36)

At the first mention of the Korean War, Chance's mood
shifts from one of remembering how the town 'buzzed with
excitement' each time he returned from his stage and film
adventures to the reality of the danger that awaited him.
He, much like Tom Wingfield in *The Glass Menagerie* who has
returned from the Merchant Marines to remember his
regrets, is afflicted by this experience. Chance perhaps
imagined that the Navy would be a glorious adventure as
depicted in films, such as those starring Victor Mature (one
of Chance's heroes as we discover in Act Two, Scene Two).
What he discovers, however, is that he could not cope with
the pressures of war. Although initially he blames his failure
to complete his tour of duty on 'the goddam routine,
discipline', he reveals that his medical discharge was the
result of a much more serious problem:

> I started to have bad dreams. Nightmares and cold sweats at
> night, and I had palpitations, and on my leave I got drunk and
> woke up in strange places with faces on the next pillow I had
> never seen before. [. . .] I cracked up, my nerves did. I got a
> medical discharge out of the service and I came home in
> civvies, then it was when I noticed how different it was, the
> town and the people in it. (37)

Suffering from a debilitating fear that one day 'a bit of hot
steel' would end his life, Chance has a nervous breakdown.
Coming home, he notices that the people of St Cloud have
changed in their reaction to him, in part, because he has no
medals or visual battle wounds. In the 1950s, military
discharges were published in newspapers; hence, the people
of St Cloud would have known the cause of Chance's early
release from the service. And, being discharged for
psychological breakdown and perhaps drug and alcohol
addiction, would have been viewed with disdain by the
general public. However, what the people of St Cloud do
not see, except perhaps for Aunt Nonnie, is that Chance's
failure to become the heroic soldier is indeed one of his
more endearing qualities. When he confronts Tom Junior in

Act Two, Scene Two, he draws a distinction between himself and Boss Finley: 'He was just called down from the hills to preach hate. I was born here to make love' (79–80). Although Chance's love-making has resulted in pain and destruction, unlike the Tom Juniors and Boss Finleys of the world, Chance is not fit to fight even for self-preservation. In the play's conclusion, he cannot strike Del Lago after she verbally cuts him down nor can he fight off Tom Junior's thugs. His fate is sealed.

Chance's naval experience is also possibly what sets his thinking apart from that of the closed-minded folk of St Cloud. Two years before the onset of the Korean War, the armed forces implemented a desegregation policy. Starting in 1948, white Americans in the Navy and other branches of the US military worked side by side with black Americans and other soldiers of colour. When Scotty tells Chance that the Youth for Tom Finley clan 'picked out a nigger at random and castrated the bastard to show they mean business about white women's protection in this state', Chance responds, 'You know what that is, don't you? Sex-envy is what that is, and the revenge for sex-envy which is a widespread disease that I have run into personally too often for me to doubt its existence or any manifestation' (70–1). Chance's diagnosis may not be psychologically or socially correct in the world outside this play, but for the audience who has witnessed Boss Finley's sexual and political potency waning Chance's definition appears right on the mark.

'The enemy time'
'Tennessee Williams's writing reveals a striking preoccupation with the problem of time,' as Mary Ann Carrigan rightly posits (221). Like Carrigan, other scholars have written about the theme of the passing of time in Williams's plays. *Sweet Bird of Youth* is no exception. Alycia Smith-Howard and Greta Heintzelman assert that the primary theme of *Sweet Bird of Youth* is decay and claim that to attempt to flee the inevitable process of ageing, Chance Wayne returns to St Cloud 'to retrieve his youth by

rekindling an innocent relationship and time in his life'
(293). In his attempt to rekindle his first love, Chance
devises a plan to blackmail the Princess into staging a
contest which he and Heavenly will win. This contest 'to
show [her] faith in YOUTH' (40) never materialises despite
the empathy Del Lago feels for Chance.

Later, in Act Two, Chance's tactics to show the town of
St Cloud that he is somebody change. After popping pills
and drinking vodka, he brags to Scotty and Bud that Del
Lago has signed a contract, giving him the lead role in a film
called 'Youth' (73). Immediately, Scotty and Bud point out
the ridiculousness of the title, seeing through Chance's lies.
However, Chance's fantastical schemes reveal that he still
buys into the Hollywood dream of glamour and youth. The
movie camera, unlike the snapshots Chance took of
Heavenly, capturing and immortalising her young body,
threatens to frame and for ever reflect back one's ageing
body as Del Lago reveals to Chance in Act One. Ultimately,
his efforts to regain his youth are met with devastating
failure. His own fall from innocence has infected Heavenly's
body. Despite Chance's desperate attempt to retrieve his
youth, like that of Alexandra Del Lago's comeback and Boss
Finley's rally, there is no turning back the clock. Even the
act of cutting out the rot decaying Heavenly's body does not
leave her unscarred. No longer a symbol of virtue, Heavenly
speaks of herself as a corpse: 'The embalmers must have
done a good job on me, Papa' (52). Williams, in essence,
reveals that there is no way to turn back the clock, no way to
wipe the slate clean, and thus there is no redemption to be
had. The passing of time, as he writes in 'The Catastrophe
of Success', is 'Loss, loss, loss, unless you devote your heart
to its opposite' (*Glass Menagerie*, 105).

Chance's struggle to stave off time is not unique.
Alexandra Del Lago and Boss Finley also fear the 'tick-tick'
of time which threatens to expose the 'burnt-out pieces' (97)
each character has become, and although Heavenly also is a
victim of time, she, unlike the others, is resigned to its
devastating cruelty. Both Chance and Boss Finley, like Del
Lago, a fugitive of her last screen debut in which the

camera's close-up exposed her age, are in a desperate battle against time. Boss Finley's mistress reveals that he can no longer 'cut the mustard' sexually (50), and his extreme and out-of-date politics lead him to resort to violence in the struggle to maintain his power. Chance, never having made it in Hollywood, relies on his good looks to latch on to wealthy and powerful women to pay his bills, but does so with the knowledge that his hair is thinning and that that which makes him attractive to these women is fading. Heavenly, he believes, is his only way to recapture and maintain his youth. However, she, too, has become 'an old childless woman' (56) after her hysterectomy.

At the play's conclusion, the audience realises that Williams's 'sweet bird of youth' is yet another myth – a myth that according to Williams we have become infected by. Nearing the tragic end of the play, Chance and Del Lago hear '*The sound of a clock ticking ... louder and louder*'. To this, Chance responds:

> It goes tick-tick, it's quieter than your heartbeat, but it's slow dynamite, a gradual explosion, blasting the world we lived in to burnt-out pieces . . . Time – who could beat it, who could defeat it ever? Maybe some saints and heroes, but not Chance Wayne. I lived on something, that – time? (97)

And continues after a brief affirmation from the Princess:

> Gnaws away, like a rat gnaws off its own foot caught in a trap, and then, with its foot gnawed off and the rat set free, couldn't run, couldn't go, bled and died. (98)

Chance's description of 'the enemy, time, in all of us' is grotesque and violent. Time as a gradual explosion turning all humankind into burnt-out scraps conveys images of war. Time wages a slow war on the body and mind; it turns us into nothing more than refuse eaten by flames. His second metaphor, one equally violent, relates to the way in which the characters feel trapped. Caught in this trap called life, Chance reveals that the destruction of time is an act of self-mutilation. Yet the violence we inflict on ourselves in an attempt to flee the ticking of the clock is futile. While Chance's return to St Cloud, his drug and alcohol abuse

and his sexual encounters may at times allow him to ignore
the passing of time, ultimately, as he reveals, attempts to flee
merely result in paralysis. Moreover, the image of the rat
gnawing off its foot suggests that he has already castrated
himself. Although the physical mutilation that will occur offstage will be committed by Tom Junior and his gang,
Chance admits that as a result of the choices he has made
he is already maimed.

Good Friday and Easter

Williams makes the setting of *Sweet Bird of Youth*, 'an Easter
Sunday, from late morning to late night', explicit
throughout. From the opening of the play when Fly, the
room-service attendant, tells Chance that 'it's *Easter* Sunday'
(8) to Boss Finley's closing political speech, Williams
continually reminds the audiences of the religious holiday
during which the action takes place. Although the play takes
place during Easter, the significance is anything but obvious.
The audience might reasonably await a resurrection and
renewal of sorts. However, Williams exploits the audience's
expectations, simultaneously revealing the way in which
Christianity itself is exploited. Boss Finley, on numerous
occasions, uses religion, particularly Good Friday and
Easter Sunday, to attempt to elevate his status as well as to
hurt Miss Lucy. The crucifixion and resurrection of Jesus
Christ becomes a tool, and, in certain circumstances, a
weapon for those attempting to maintain or seize power.
Boss Finley first employs the image of Christ's crucifixion
after he is attacked by Tom Junior about his relations with
Miss Lucy: 'Mind your own goddam business. A man with a
mission, which he holds sacred, and on the strength of
which he rises to high public office – crucified in this way,
publicly, by his own offspring' (51). Using the rhetoric of
religious doctrine, Boss Finley sets himself up as a Christ-like
figure, crucified by his son.

Having been 'crucified' by his lover as well, Boss Finley
seeks revenge on Miss Lucy. When Miss Lucy first appears
with her finger bandaged, she relates to Stuff the extent of

Boss Finley's cruelty. Boss Finley, she explains, brought her a candy Easter egg with a jewellery box inside it. When she opened the Easter egg and the jewellery box, she found a lovely diamond pin inside, but as she was about to remove the pin, 'the old son of a bitch slam[med] the lid of the box on [her] fingers' (59). Disguising his 'weapon' in a candy Easter egg, Boss Finley masks his violent nature. While at times seemingly sweet and generous to Miss Lucy, unlike Christ he does not forgive and he is not afraid to punish those who threaten his sexual and political image.

Boss Finley again draws a parallel between himself and Christ during his television rally:

> Last Friday . . . Last Friday, Good Friday. I said last Friday, Good Friday . . . Quiet, may I have your attention please . . . Last Friday, Good Friday, I seen a horrible thing on the campus of our great State University, which I built for the state. A hideous strawstuffed effigy of myself, Tom Finley, was hung and set fire to in the main quadrangle of the college. This outrage was inspired . . . inspired by the Northern radical press. However, that was Good Friday. Today is Easter. I say that was Good Friday. Today is Easter Sunday and I am in St Cloud. (86)

In this passage, in which Boss Finley struggles to be heard by a crowd already stirred up by the Heckler's intrusion, the ageing politician grasps at Christian doctrine to appeal to his audience. Revealing that the youth of Florida have burned an effigy of him on Good Friday, Boss Finley attempts to position himself as a saviour whom the youth of his state, polluted by what is written in the Northern papers, cannot yet appreciate. Ending his speech (which also concludes Act Two) with 'Today is Easter Sunday and I am in St Cloud', Boss Finley evokes a resurrection, but this is a resurrection that never takes place perhaps because, although Boss Finley may attempt to fashion himself as a saviour, for Williams and his audience, this demagogue is more clearly aligned with the thieves crucified alongside Christ. Thomas Adler adds that '*Sweet Bird of Youth* ends, significantly, not on Easter morning – which is the moment of complete belief and hope – but on Easter evening,

biblically a moment of absolute doubt and challenge to faith
that can be alloyed only by dependence on experimental
proof of a resurrection' (148), but it is a resurrection that
Williams never allows for.

Williams also cheats his audience into believing that
Alexandra Del Lago and Chance Wayne might possibly be
resurrected – he cheats us into believing that there might be
a happy ending after all. Although Chance has returned to
regain his lost youth and his lost girl, his desperate attempts
are met with failure. He gains the Princess's sympathy for a
time, and with it her financial and emotional support, but
finds himself 'lost in beanstalk country, the ogre's country at
the top of the beanstalk, the country of the flesh-hungry,
blood-thirsty ogre' (77), as Del Lago so fittingly describes the
world of St Cloud and beyond. St Cloud is, indeed, a place
where 'monsters' like Tom Junior and his father seek out
and commit violent acts against those perceived as
trespassers. In the end, Chance, '*with a sort of deathbed dignity
and honesty*', resigns himself to his fate. He allows Tom
Junior, Scotty and Bud to enter the room, and as these
brutal youths surround him, he rises up to approach the
audience with his last words: 'I don't ask for your pity, but
just for your understanding – not even that – no. Just for
your recognition of me in you, and the enemy, time, in us
all' (98). By having the last lines before the curtain falls
spoken to the audience, Williams positions Chance as the
audience's messenger. Yet, rather than have this messenger
rise up triumphantly, as would be fitting for Easter, he has
Chance face his doom, his crucifixion of sorts. However,
before his castration, Chance asks his audience to recognise
that a part of him resides within us. We desire success,
youth, happiness and love, but the 'monsters' in this play
(the Finley clan and time) keep us from succeeding.

Del Lago, one of the few characters who sympathises with
Chance, knows very well how hard it is to succeed in this
monstrous world. In the last act, it is tempting to associate
the Easter resurrection with Del Lago's comeback,
especially after she discovers that her last film has 'broken
box-office records' and been called 'the greatest comeback

in the history of the industry' (94). Yet, even Del Lago does
not believe that her rebirth as a film star will last. While
nothing in Del Lago's dialogue gives her doubts away,
Williams reveals that the Princess, even after her bitter
argument with Chance, again tries to convince him to leave
with her because she knows her fame will be short-lived:

> *The report from Sally Powers may be and probably is a factually accurate
> report; but to indicate she is going on to further triumph would be to falsify
> her future. She makes this instinctive admission to herself when she sits
> down by* **Chance** *on the bed, facing the audience. Both are faced with
> castration, and in her heart she knows it.* (97)

This knowledge of the castration she too faces is difficult for
an actress to convey. Without dialogue that designates her
doubt and lack of faith in her future, Del Lago must express
through her gestures that she is fated, as is Chance. Her
journey, Williams reveals, is one that will result in future
disappointment, flight from failure and ultimately
crucifixion without resurrection.

Cut: film and television
When Chance recalls for Del Lago and later for Aunt
Nonnie his past, the audience learns that his first attempt
to make a name for himself was on stage. His plan, like
the dreams of many actors of the 1950s, was to land roles
on Broadway (at which he is in part successful) before
heading out to Hollywood. This Hollywood dream, the
dream of seeing one's name on a screen shown across the
country, is for many a bitter nightmare. The film industry,
for Williams, has the ability to offer instant success as well
as instant failure. Del Lago testifies to this when she
bitterly says:

> Ha . . . Ha . . . The glorious comeback, when I turned fool and
> came back . . . The screen's a very clear mirror. There's a
> thing called a close-up. The camera advances and you stand
> still and your head, your face, is caught in the frame of the
> picture with a light blazing on it and all your terrible history
> screams while you smile . . . (25)

Once a star with her own fan club, Del Lago, having agreed
to come back to the movies, takes desperate flight after
hearing the audience gasp at her close-up at the film's
premiere. Oddly, her description of the close-up resembles
that of a torture sequence – a light blazing in her face as her
'terrible history screams' out. Her 'history', while in part a
reference to having aged, also reflects how she has passed
the years. There is a sense in her recollection of the
premiere that Del Lago's initial disappearance from the
Silver Screen was the result of some undesirable past
behaviour; she was, according to her own accounts of Franz
Albertzart, a diva. What she then sees and perceives others
witnessing is her past, those years she hid from the camera.
This camera, like 'a very clear mirror', reflects not only her
physical flaws but also her ethical and moral blemishes.

When Del Lago asks Chance to tell his life story as an
'audition, a sort of screen test' (35), she symbolically places a
mirror in front of him. He begins boasting about his
popularity in St Cloud and his minor successes on
Broadway, but Chance's 'screen test' begins to reflect a
troubled youth. Williams 'proposed to use the screen as the
metaphor for consciousness, a consciousness both lyrical
and philosophical – personal and public – in nature'
(Jackson, 196). While no camera or screen is present in this
scene, Chance's monologue is directed on the forestage; he
is speaking out to the audience while Del Lago, staring into
a mirror, applies her make-up. Speaking to an imaginary
camera, Chance's mood shifts as he recollects his Navy
service, his drinking, his sexual promiscuity and his other
failures, including Heavenly's attempt to push him away,
with a tragic aura. It is when he becomes sincere that he
captures the Princess's attention. 'Chance,' Del Lago
tenderly says moving away from the mirror, 'you're a lost
little boy that I really would like to help find himself' (41). At
this point, Chance awakens from the trance of the
imaginary mirror reflecting his sad life, and states
confidently, 'I passed the screen test!' For Williams, acting is
not pretending to be someone one is not; it is not just play.
He worked with method actors – actors working with

techniques of tapping into one's own past experiences to convey the emotional depth of the characters they are embodying. In acting and perhaps in writing for the screen or stage, one inadvertently expresses one's own tragedy. This is not to be mistaken with biographical interpretations of plays, that is, Williams is not staging his life over and over again in his plays. He understands, however, that an actor and a writer brings his history with him, and ultimately this is also what makes the industry so cruel. Those who cannot face the mirror that will expose their ugliness as well as beauty fail.

Williams additionally takes his pen(knife) to the television industry. Not only does the camera threaten Del Lago, exposing more than she wishes others to see, but also television allows Boss Finley, and politicians like Joe McCarthy, to stage, perform and ultimately to try to 'cut' his way to the top. Williams's technique to represent the television screen on stage warrants some note. While Stuff, Miss Lucy and Chance initially look out towards the fourth wall, where a beam of light flickers indicating the television screen, a sudden shift takes place. When Chance walks downstage, '*the whole back wall of the stage*' becomes a giant TV screen. Boss Finley is seen, larger than life, with his '*arm around Heavenly*' (84). Despite Boss Finley's attempt to use national television coverage to boost his voting public, the screen, which has the potential to manipulate time, place and circumstances (Jackson, 195–6), ultimately reveals his personal ugliness when he has the Heckler removed from the rally. Captured on screen is not just the apparently pure image of Heavenly and her proud brother and father, but also Boss Finley's inability to face his 'terrible history' – the family tragedy and his failing political pull is captured on the public screen/mirror. If, as Roland Barthes argues, what politicians attempt to create when they appear in front of a camera is an image that their public recognises within themselves,[3] then here the public sees its own racism and sexism. Williams asks his

---

[3] *Mythologies*, trans. Annette Lavers, New York, Hill and Wang, 1972, p. 91.

audience to see the stage as a mirror of an America
polluted by narrow-minded Boss Finleys. However,
Williams incites his audience with an urge to rid America
of such ugliness – the ugliness of the HUAC, of a
segregated South and of a homophobic nation.

Structure, language and style

Structure

While the structure of *Sweet Bird of Youth* often has been
criticised as clumsy and disjointed, it pulls together private
and public anxieties concerning age, the loss of power and
the fear of the 'other' through spacial arenas. The play is set
in two main spaces – the hotel's bedroom and lounge and
the terrace of the Finley home. These spaces interestingly
blur the distinction between the private and public, as does
Boss Finley who uses his children to further his political
means. Jo Mielziner's original set design in which the hotel
bedroom was present in each act realises this breakdown of
the personal and political tragedies in *Sweet Bird of Youth*.
The structure and the set design ultimately bring together
the stories of Chance and Del Lago, Chance and Heavenly,
and the political turmoil of the South.

Sweet Bird of Youth takes a great deal from Greek tragedy.
Despite the various locations, the play, like those of the
Greeks, takes place in one day 'from late morning till late
night'. As the play continues, the dramatic urgency
intensifies until the tragic end. The tragedy, in *Sweet Bird of
Youth* as in Greek drama, lies in the downfall of a larger-than-
life character. Williams interestingly depicts the downfall of
three demigods – Alexandra Del Lago who is in exile after
her fall, Chance Wayne whose boasting elevates his status to
a monumental gigolo and Boss Finley whose bellowing at
rallies cannot stop his political power from coming to an end.
Both Boss Finley and Chance are sacrificed within the action
of the play. Chance's castration (though never enacted on
stage) is more than brutality; it is a ritualistic cutting to send
a warning to those who threaten the social structure of St

Cloud. Boss Finley's rally is disrupted in the same manner as it had been before; the repetition in method and of questions transforms the event into a ritualistic roasting.

Language

Williams's writing is often described as poetic. His use of metaphors, symbols, repetition, dialect and slang help to construct the vivid worlds he stages. Embodying his central characters, Chance and Del Lago, with a language rich in images borrowed from children's fairytales, images of insects, rats and other animals gnawing at abstractions such as time, and endowing them with lengthy personal histories, Williams elevates their status. Chance and Del Lago are not only given the most lines but their use of language also reveals that these two figures are dreamers, rich in imaginative power and longing to create personas on the Silver Screen. They, like Boss Finley, are hyper-aware of the audience, speaking always as if they are performing. Along with the rich images that Chance conjures up, he turns to the auditorium, speaking to the audience in Act One, Scene Two, when he recalls the life he has led, and in Act Three when he is about to face castration. Unlike Boss Finley whose speeches are disrupted, Chance's are observed in silence, much like those of a Shakespearean hero.

The use of slang and dialect in *Sweet Bird of Youth* is often associated with the antagonists. Tom Junior and his father speak with strong southern accents, often leaving off the endings to words. Although they know how to use language to perpetuate their racist ideologies, ultimately for an educated audience, their dialect and slang signal their barbarism. Tom Junior, for example, uses profanity such as 'ruttin' and shows little respect to his elders. Williams aligns the way in which a character speaks with his temperament.

Plastic theatre

In his production notes for *The Glass Menagerie*, Williams wrote of a form of theatre that he hoped would take hold on the American stage. Plastic theatre, as he called this form, was an attempt to create theatre in which 'truth, life, or reality is an organic thinking which poetic imagination can represent or suggest, in essence, only through changing into other forms than those which were merely present in appearance'. Leaving behind realist conventions which had all too much dominated the American stage, Williams created a dramatic form which merged a poetic, lyric quality with popular appeal. His revolutionary concept of plastic theatre merged non-verbal expressions to illuminate the dialogue and textual version of the play. In *Sweet Bird of Youth*, Williams achieves this new dramatic form through his use of symbols, as seen in the gulls, the recurring musical composition called the 'Lament' and the use of a cyclorama on which 'nonrealistic projections' 'should give a poetic unity of mood to the several specific settings' (5).

Before any word is uttered on stage, the audience hears '*the soft, urgent cries of birds, [and] the sound of their wings*' (7). Immediately, Williams signals to the audience that this play is about an urgency to soar above one's status and to flee one's failures. After this, Fly, the black man who provides room-service at the Royal Palms Hotel, appears with vodka, another form of escape. This minor character, only seen briefly, reminds the audience that, like Chance, he is stuck in a dead-end job in a racist Southern town which will viciously cut him if he is caught on the street after midnight.

The gulls appear again immediately after Chance learns of his mother's death: '**Chance** *slowly turns his back on the man and crosses to the window. Shadows of birds sweep the blind. He lowers it a little before he turns back to* **Scudder**' (10). They reappear only a few pages later, after Scudder has left and once Alexandra Del Lago has woken from her drunken sleep. While Del Lago attempts to figure out where she is and with whom she shares her bed, the audience sees '*Gulls fly past window, shadows sweeping the blind: they cry out with soft urgency*' (21). These birds are not 'birds of youth', frolicking and singing in the sun without cares. In both instances, the shadows of their wings signal a desire to flee, yet an inability to escape. The gulls stay near the sea, as Chance does, because the ocean is their home; however, it is a home that is bound up with uncertainty and danger. What lies beneath the water is unknown. The cries of these gulls, moreover, are not sweet, like the cooing of pigeons. Del Lago remarks that they sound like 'pigeons with laryngitis' (21). Their hoarse cries are filled with a panic-stricken urgency which is mirrored in Chance and the Princess.

Although Williams's positioning of the gulls is not as specific later in the play, the terrifying cries of these birds are ever-present in Act Two, Scene One. '*The Gulf,*' he writes, '*is suggested by the brightness and the gulls crying as in Act One*' (43). Here the gulls heighten the audience's awareness of Boss Finley's desperate attempt to maintain his political power and to re-establish the respect he once held in his family. When told that his mistress, Miss Lucy, has exposed his ageing and no longer virile body, Boss Finley is '*wounded, baffled*' (51). Indeed, the description 'baffled' is used in conjunction with Boss Finley again when he watches his daughter shortly after.

The ever-present cries of the gulls, moreover, reflect Heavenly's tragedy. Rendered barren by her hysterectomy, she has become a corpse. When asked where Heavenly is, her brother, Tom Junior says, 'She's lyin' out on the beach like a dead body washed up on it' (46). Williams asks us to imagine the beauty, washed up on the shore, as gulls frantically swoop down and devour her much like Boss Finley who insists that she escort him in his television appearance in a 'stainless white' dress 'to scotch these rumors about your corruption' (56). But by putting Heavenly in the public eye, Boss Finley exposes her to the Heckler's and by extension the viewing public's vicious pecking.

Apart from the '*Mozartian music, suggesting a court dance*' (52), which was cut from the production of the play and the popular tunes sung in the bar during Act Two, Scene Two, the only music in *Sweet Bird of Youth* is the 'Lament', or 'Lamentation' as it is sometimes called. Although this piece of music was composed specifically for the play by Williams's old friend Paul Bowles, author of *The Sheltering Sky*, the 'Lament' has a long tradition in the arts. It is one of

the oldest poetic expressions of grief, regret and sorrow in
Western music. In Baroque opera, the Lament is often an
aria sung by the leading lady. Williams's 'Lament', heard
seven times during the play, serves a similar purpose. When
this composition is heard, Chance is hopeless. Towards the
end of Act One, Scene One, as Chance's situation becomes
increasingly desperate, the Lament makes its first
appearance. From this moment, we understand Chance's
attempt to blackmail the Princess Kosmonopolis is an act of
desperation – not an act of greed but a struggle to regain his
lost youth by winning over the girl he loved. The Lament,
however, also signals that his plan will backfire. Despite his
attempt to make the ageing actress submit to him, he will
have to submit to Alexandra Del Lago before the end of Act
One. After the Lament begins again, Del Lago softly tells
Chance that she needs

> that distraction. It's time for me to find out if you're able to
> give it to me. You mustn't hang onto your silly little idea that
> you can increase your value by turning away and looking out a
> window when somebody wants you . . . I want you . . . I say
> now and I mean now, then and not until then will I call
> downstairs and tell the hotel cashier that I'm sending a young
> man down with some travelers' checks to cash for me . . . (33)

Attempting to shame the Princess into signing her cheques,
he in turn is shamed as he becomes her gigolo. The Lament
arises early on in Scene Two of the First Act. Full of regret
and sorrow for his shameful sexual act, Chance now reveals
more than his current desperation. He reveals his entire
lamentable history.

The Lament is not heard again until Act Two, Scene
Two, after Tom Junior confronts Chance with Heavenly's
tragedy. In response to Tom Junior's charge that Chance
passed on a venereal disease which he contracted after
sleeping with 'Minnie, that slept with any goddam gigolo
bastard she could pick up on Bourbon Street or the docks',
Chance says, 'I left town before I found out I –' (81). Here,
the Lament signals Chance's sorrow at discovering he has
infected Heavenly, and that, as a result, Heavenly was
operated on. The Lament may also signal his regret for not

contacting her once he knew of his own diseased body. If
Heavenly had known and if the disease had been diagnosed
early on, she would have been spared being 'spayed like a
dawg by Dr George Scudder's knife'. The Lament, here,
works to draw out sympathy for Chance. While his actions
are not commendable, he does feel sorrow and regret.

As Chance returns to the Princess, who has since
ventured downstairs in a dishevelled and drugged state,
'*"The Lament" is in the air. It blends with the wind-blown sound of
the palms*'. It is at this moment that the Lament is clearly
defined. Del Lago describes it as a feeling of loss:

> All day I've kept hearing a sort of lament that drifts through
> the air of this place. It says, 'Lost, lost, never to be found
> again.' Palm gardens by the sea and olive groves on
> Mediterranean islands all have that lament drifting through
> them. 'Lost, lost' . . . The isle of Cyprus, Monte Carlo, San
> Remo, Torremolenas, Tangiers. They're all places of exile
> from whatever we loved. Dark glasses, wide-brimmed hats and
> whispers, 'Is that her?' Shocked whispers . . . Oh, Chance,
> believe me, after failure comes flight. Nothing ever comes after
> failure but flight. Face it. Call the car, have them bring down
> the luggage and let's go on along the Old Spanish Trail. (*She
> tries to hold him.*) (82)

While St Cloud is initially a place of exile for the Princess,
the whispers begin to haunt her, revealing that she must flee
again. But more importantly, she recognises before Chance
does that his comeback has been a failure. His only chance
of escaping bodily harm, she knows, is flight. For Chance, St
Cloud was once an exile from his failure to become a film
star but now it is his doom.

During the play's last moments in Act Three, the Lament
returns signalling Chance's doom. After the frightening visit
Tom Junior and his clan pay to Del Lago, she reminds
Chance that he was the one who 'put such rot in
[Heavenly's] body she had to be gutted and hung on a
butcher's hook, like a chicken dressed for Sunday'. Hearing
this, initially aiming at the Princess, he '*strikes down at his own
belly and he bends double with a sick cry. Palm Garden wind: whisper
of "The Lament"*' (95). And only a few moments later when

Chance is resolved to face his castration, the Lament fades in and continues for the remainder of the play (97). The echo of 'lost, lost, lost' is crucial here. Not only is Chance about to lose his virility, but he recognises that he has lost his youthfulness, his hope and his will to go on. His acceptance of his fate is almost honourable.

The settings, Williams urges, 'should be treated as freely and sparingly as the sets for *Cat on a Hot Tin Roof* or *Summer and Smoke*' (3). Murphy confirms that the Broadway premiere of *Sweet Bird of Youth* did indeed resemble *Cat on a Hot Tin Roof*, with a bed occupying a large part of the playing field. Furthermore, no walls or doors were constructed on stage; all the doors and windows were mimed. The spaces were non-realistic as they ran into one another. Even during the bar-room scene, for example, the bedroom was partly visible. To suggest this non-realistic, fluid space, the cyclorama at the rear of the stage was essential as it conveyed 'shutters in the first scene and palms, sea, and sky when the "shutters" were "opened"' (Murphy, 145). In his 'Setting and Special Effects', Williams stressed that 'During the daytime scenes the cyclorama projection is a poetic abstraction of semitropical sea and sky in fair spring weather. At night it is the Palm Garden with its branches among the stars' (3). The focus on the non-realistic, the abstract, moves this play away from realist conventions in which the setting or projections would reflect the current turmoil of the characters. Instead, Williams uses the cyclorama to create a contrast between the lives of Chance and the Princess, and the seemingly peaceful outside world. The beauty of the palm garden and the sea remind the viewers just how artificial such hotel settings are. In other words, the world Chance and Del Lago live in is brutal; it only appears to be calm and beautiful. Moreover, the image of the palm branches among the stars is symbolic. While never reaching the stars, the night shadows give the illusion of reaching for the unobtainable. Chance's attempt to reach for Heaven(ly) – is an impossibility.

Southern Gothic
Sweet Bird of Youth is an example of Southern Gothic, which
draws on the Gothic tradition of nineteenth-century
England that, among other traits, questions whether
monstrous outcasts are truly monstrous – as seen in Mary
Shelley's *Frankenstein* (1839). A key feature of Southern
Gothic is the plight of ostracised and oppressed individuals,
such as blacks, homosexuals, women and Northerners, who
were deemed dangerous to the fragile antebellum South. In
Sweet Bird of Youth, while all the characters are damaged and
delusional (another feature of Southern Gothic), Williams
succeeds in stirring up panic and sympathy for Chance
whose fate parallels the story of a black man castrated by
Tom Junior and his Youth for Tom Finley clan. Chance is
the ostracised Other who threatens the stability of St Cloud
because his presence is a constant reminder of the
corruption and pollution eating away at the community.

Characters

Despite his previous successes with creating vivid characters
such as Tom and Amanda Wingfield in *The Glass Menagerie*,
Blanche and Stanley in *A Streetcar Named Desire*, Maggie and
Brick in *Cat on a Hot Tin Roof,* among other notable
characters, Tennessee Williams was never quite satisfied
with the characters of *Sweet Bird of Youth*. Although he 'was
deeply interested in the two main characters [Chance and
Del Lago]', he told *Manchester Guardian Weekly*'s W. J.
Weatherby in 1959, 'the other characters did not have the
same interest for me' (quoted in Devlin, 60). He felt
particularly dissatisfied with Boss Finley. The power of *Sweet
Bird of Youth* rests in the two main characters' struggle
against a world of hateful and cruel monsters.

Chance Wayne
Although Williams was interested in the development of
Chance Wayne, more than a decade after the play opened

on Broadway he was still unsatisfied with this 'hustler hero
of *Sweet Bird of Youth*' (Clum, 128). In a 1971 interview with
Jeanne Fayard, Williams expressed that he never felt that
Chance was an effective character. He went on to explain
that Chance

> is used in a symbolic manner. It [his castration] is a ritualistic
> death, a metaphor. He had to be real to be important. You
> cannot use a character as a dramatic symbol if he is important.
> You cannot use a character as a dramatic symbol if he is not
> first real to you. I didn't discover his real value until the end.
> (Quoted in Devlin, 211)

For his audiences, however, Chance is much more than a
symbol. The play's intrigue is partly a result of the empathy
that characters like Chance evoke in viewers. We see
ourselves, or at least our dreams, in his struggle to be
famous and his failure to achieve that success. This
particular myth, rooted in the American consciousness,
commonly referred to as 'the American Dream', recalls a
tradition depicted in American Realist novels such as
Theodore Dreiser's *An American Tragedy* (1925). Like Clyde,
the protagonist of Dreiser's novel, Chance strives to rise
above his poverty and in doing so compromises ethical and
moral codes. In *Sweet Bird of Youth*, however, the gigolo's
failure does not leave the audience with a moral lesson. For
Williams, those who succeed and those who do not are no
more or less virtuous than the other characters struggling to
make a name for themselves.

Furthermore, Williams reveals that the American dream,
or the Cinderella story, turns individuals into monsters. This
is clearly seen when Chance, struggling to capture the
attention and trust of the bar-room crowd in Act Two, is
suddenly faced with Del Lago. High on drugs and alcohol,
the Princess, having felt something for Chance when he
confessed his failures to her in Act One, Scene Two,
ventures to find him so that they can escape the doom she
feels approaching in St Cloud. Alone and seeking comfort
from him in the flight she wishes for them both, she pleads,
'Don't leave me. If you do I'll turn into the monster again.

I'll be the first lady of the Beanstalk Country' (82). Chance, however, does not soften to her desperate appeal. Instead, '*in [his own] desperation*', he calls out, 'Wheel chair! . . . Wheel chair! Stuff, get the lady a wheel chair! She's having another attack!' While Chance's inability to care for Del Lago in her moment of despair is undoubtedly cruel, it is important to note that at this very moment he is desperate to regain his reputation and his youth. He is consumed with a dream which has infected him like the disease he has put into Heavenly's body, rotting away his moral and ethical responses and transforming him into a monster – cruel and selfish, ready to destroy those in his way.

Chance is much more complicated than Williams realised. While he displays cruelty when desperate, he is quite tender and lovable when he remembers his failures. When reminiscing with Aunt Nonnie about his first stage appearance at 'a lousy national contest', he finally lets his guard down after trying to convince himself that they won a prize:

> We would have won it, but I blew my lines. Yes, I that put on and produced the damn thing, couldn't even hear the damn lines being hissed at me by that fat girl with the book in the wings. (*He buries his face in his hands.*) (63)

Aunt Nonnie here speaks for the audience: 'I loved you for that, son, and so did Heavenly, too.' These moments of weakness, vulnerability and honesty set Chance apart from the cruel inhabitants of St Cloud.

Williams's genius as a playwright lies in his ability to stir sympathy for Chance, to transform this tainted man who lacks moral fibre into a hero of sorts. Despite his bad choices, selfishness and bravado, among other vices, Chance is wronged; the audience does not want this faded golden boy to be castrated.

Alexandra Del Lago

Alexandra Del Lago is notably one of Williams's complex and memorable female characters. This ageing, washed-up movie star is at times a self-proclaimed 'monster'. In her heyday, she was a diva, breaking the careers of young men like Franz Albertzart: 'I had to fire him. He held me too tight in the waltz scene, his anxious fingers left bruises once so violent, they, they dislocated a disc in my spine' (90). Even after her return to the screen, a return she believes has been a failure, she asserts her power over young men. In her flight, she uses beach boys like Chance to distract her from the harsh reality that '*she is equally doomed. She can't turn back the clock any more than can* **Chance***, and the clock is equally relentless to them both*' (96–7). Her ability to devour and destroy men is, according to Chance, an act of emasculation. When Del Lago tries to convince Chance to leave with her in the final act, reminding him that if he stays he will be castrated, Chance says, 'You did that to me this morning, here on this bed, where I had the honor, where I had the great honor . . .' (95). However, her acts of emasculating men are not out of 'sex-envy', bigotry or hate. Rather, her acts are tied to her vanity – her longing for youth. Like Chance, she seeks to blind herself to the ticking of the clock through sexual unions with the young.

Del Lago is not simply a frustrated monster, seeking the admiring gaze of her fans and the 'hairless, silky-smooth gold' (18) bodies of young men. She is, as Williams's agent asserted about all Williams's female characters, an ordinary woman. Recalling an encounter with a group of angry women after the premiere of *Summer and Smoke*, Williams writes that they asked, 'Why do you always write about frustrated women?' (*Where I Live*, 26). His agent, Margo Jones, rescued him from the confrontation. Williams recalls that Jones told these women, 'Tennessee does not write about abnormal characters!' He writes about 'People!' Alexandra Del Lago is very real, complete with grand neuroses and the means temporarily to forget them. At times monstrous, the Princess is also a vulnerable, frightened animal. She does not stick around to fight her battles, but runs until all is clear. While we often see the Princess bossing Chance around, calling his bluff and ridiculing his pathetic attempt to blackmail her, Del Lago also displays moments of vulnerability. In Act One, Scene Two, she is touched by Chance's life story (perhaps because it is similar to her own). In the following act, she stumbles into the bar, drunk and high, but ready to admit that Chance has made her feel something for someone other than herself. And in Act Three, after her encouraging phone call with Sally Powers, Del Lago, revealing her own vulnerability, again identifies with Chance:

> In both **Chance** *and the* **Princess**, *we should return to the huddling together of the lost, but not with sentiment, which is false, but with whatever is truthful in the moments when people share doom, face firing squads together.* (96)

Regardless of the positive reviews of her comeback, Del Lago knows her success will not last.

Her alias, the Princess Kosmonopolis, likewise points to the complexity of Del Lago's character. Not merely a diva, struggling to survive in the movie industry that turned her into a monster, her alias leads back to Williams's discussion of the 'Cinderella story' as well as suggesting that before being consumed by this Hollywood dream, she was capable of kindness, generosity and grace – traits that in fairytales lead the princess to winning her prince. However, in the modern age, even when this princess displays kindness and generosity, she is ultimately unable to transform or for that matter save Chance. The pseudonym, furthermore, reflects her past. Like Chance (and Cinderella who cleaned and toiled for her step-sisters), Del Lago was not always rich and famous. She began, like them, with only beauty to boast of. The power struggle between Chance and Del Lago is, in part, fuelled by their recognition of their similarities. Chance could easily have reaped the benefits of fame as Del Lago does and she could easily have remained paralysed in her poverty.

Boss Finley

Tennessee Williams revealed that for him it was important to like his characters, but to like Boss Finley was impossible

(Gunn, 27). Never quite satisfied, Williams allowed Elia Kazan to develop the Boss Finley sections for the 1959 Broadway debut of *Sweet Bird of Youth*. Kazan softened the tyrant considerably, transforming him into a sincere politician and loving father (Parker, par. 18). However, when Williams revised the play for publication in 1960–1, he omitted many of Kazan's additions (Parker, par. 1), leaving contemporary readers and viewers with a portrait of a 'hateful political and domestic bully' (Parker, par. 18).

Nevertheless, Boss Finley's desperate struggle to survive the changes occurring in the modern world, a struggle against time, makes him more than just a political and domestic tyrant. Indeed, there is an unmistakable resemblance between Boss Finley and *Cat on a Hot Tin Roof*'s Big Daddy, as Brenda Murphy and other scholars point out. However, unlike Big Daddy who is an 'epic figure, an icon of masculinity, vitality, and power',[4] Boss Finley is not bestowed with 'a kingly magnitude', a description given to Big Daddy by the playwright in his *Memoirs*. While Big Daddy, like Boss Finley, is a domineering father who is desperately trying to maintain his patriarchal position within the family, he, unlike Boss Finley, is just and kind as is notable in his behaviour towards Maggie. Although a hateful figure, Boss Finley is much more complex than the bigoted and corrupt politician Williams thought him. A hillbilly, according to himself and Miss Lucy, he is perhaps a victim of his own environment and upbringing. He is not an educated man, although he has helped to build the state's university. Despite being one of the founders of this institution, his attitude towards education is mixed. Although he is humiliated by Tom Junior's having 'flunked out of college with grades that only a moron would have an excuse for', Boss Finley does not value the process of learning. He aids his son in being readmitted 'by fake examinations, answers provided beforehand, stuck in your fancy pockets' (50). Helping his son to cheat his way back into college, Boss Finley reveals that his corruption goes

---

[4] *Cat on a Hot Tin Roof*, commentary by Philip C. Kolin, p. xxxix.

beyond pocketing oil money; it has infected every institution of Florida.

Boss Finley will go to great lengths to create the illusion of a happy and successful family. Along with attempting to create the illusion of his son's intellectual integrity, he also attempts to mask the tragedy of his daughter's venereal disease. Initially he tries to cover up her operation. Even after promoting Dr Scudder to chief surgeon and arranging a marriage between the two (a marriage that has not yet taken place), Boss Finley fails to keep Heavenly's secret. Forcing his daughter to join him at the Youth for Tom Finley televised rally to represent white purity, he believes that 'lookin' at you [Heavenly], all in white like a virgin, nobody would dare to speak or believe the ugly stories about you' (56). However, he is not really concerned about his daughter's reputation or feelings nor is he concerned about Tom Junior's obscene behaviour. He ultimately uses his children: his concern is his own reputation and the winning of the next election. He is afraid that the scandals surrounding his children will 'defeat the mission' to eradicate 'all of them that want to adulterate the pure white blood of the South' (57).

These extreme attempts to hide his family's failures reflect Boss Finley's awareness of his loss of power, both in the home and in the political arena. Angry and frustrated with Tom Junior, he says,

> It's a curious thing, a mighty peculiar thing, how often a man that rises to high public office is drug back down by every soul he harbors under his roof. He harbors them under his roof, and they pull the roof down on him. Every last living one of them. (49)

During their family dispute, Boss Finley and his son are described as '*two stags*', prepared to buck each other. The description is one that leads back to masculinity and power. Boss Finley, being the older 'stag', is bound to lose. He can no longer maintain the alpha position, as seen when the hillbilly heckler disrupts the rally. The Heckler unsettles Boss Finley, not by attacking his politics in an objective

debate, but by targeting Boss Finley's greatest wound –
Heavenly's impurity.

Heavenly Finley
At the opening of the play, Fly, the bellboy, speaks of
Heavenly and Chance's young love. Having been a waiter
in the Grand Ballroom years ago, he tells Chance that he
used to see him 'with that real pretty girl you used to dance
so good with, Mr Boss Finley's daughter' (8). While this
reference to Heavenly seems insignificant at first, as Act
One progresses the audience discovers that Chance has
returned for the young Heavenly whose photograph he
carries around with him. This photograph both reveals what
she once was to Chance and what she has become. A nude
image of a fifteen-year-old girl with the tide 'beginning to
lap over her body like it desired her like [Chance] did and
still [does] and will always, always' (38), the photograph
signifies youth and Chance's desire to possess that youth.
The water lapping over Heavenly's body, furthermore,
preps the audience for another destructive image. In Act
Two, Scene One, she stops and contemplates a fern
ravished by the wind. Like the delicate fern '*that the salty Gulf
wind has stripped nearly bare*' (53), the salt water of the Gulf of
Mexico symbolises the process of decay. Heavenly, while
only fifteen in the photograph, has already been sexually
involved with Chance – an involvement which is the end of
her purity and innocence.

   Photographs are mere traces, shadowy figments, of the
individual photographed. As a reproduction of Heavenly,
the photograph signifies the hollowness of this idealised
image which Chance carries around with him. She, as Clum
astutely describes, is 'a mirage, the shell of the girl Chance
loved' (140). Not only is the photograph a false image of the
Heavenly that we meet in the second act, but it is also only a
trace of what she once was. She is, indeed, washed up on
the shore like a shell, or as Tom Junior more crudely puts it,
'She's lyin' out on the beach like a dead body washed up on
it' (46). Several of the play's characters, including Heavenly

herself, refer to her body as dead, gutted and old. Defeated, Heavenly apologises to her father for the embarrassment her hysterectomy causes him but reveals that her own pain exceeds his:

> I felt worse than embarrassed when I found out that Dr George Scudder's knife had cut the youth out of my body, made me an old childless woman. Dry, cold, empty, like an old woman. (55–6)

Acknowledging her own emptiness, she cannot be anything more to Chance than an empty, hollow dream –a mirage in desolate Beanstalk Country.

Tom Junior

While Boss Finley represents politically charged hatred and bigotry, his son, Tom Junior, is perhaps more despicable. He has been the subject of many scandals. Without the help of his father's corrupt methods, Tom Junior would not have been to college. Furthermore, he has received newspaper coverage for 'drunk drivin'' and 'once for a stag party' that cost Boss Finley a considerable amount of money to 'hush it up' (49). Despite the supposed justice he seeks for his sister, Tom Junior is not concerned with Heavenly's well-being. His actions are motivated by his own loss of pride; like his father he has been shamed by her sexual relationship with Chance, an individual whose own conduct is questionable. For Tom Junior, his sister contracted a whore's disease, and thus she has tainted the family's reputation.

The leader of a small gang of thugs, Tom Junior employs his father's name to commit acts of violence that are motivated by racism, 'sex-envy' and pride. The Youth for Tom Finley clubs, endorsed by Boss Finley, are a sadistic and immoral lot. Tom Junior and his gang are responsible for randomly picking out a black man and castrating him 'to show they mean business about white women's protection in this state' (70). Regardless of the rhetoric Tom Junior and his gang use to condone their actions, these acts are not carried out to 'protect' white women. These acts, including

Tom Junior's threat to castrate Chance if he does not leave
town, are tied to his own emasculation. As the Finley empire
is challenged, Tom Junior and his father resort to desperate
and violent deeds. He and Boss Finley are envious of those
who are gaining power – both in the political arena and in
the private one. Having corrupted his sister, Chance
represents the encroaching threat to Tom Junior's power.
He no longer has control over his little sister's behaviour.
With his masculinity in jeopardy, Tom Junior resorts to
lashing out at those whom he perceives as holding power
over women.

Miss Lucy

An opportunist, Miss Lucy, like Alexandra Del Lago, uses
men. While Del Lago uses Chance to distract her from what
she believes has been a failed comeback and from the
destructive forces of time, Miss Lucy in essence prostitutes
herself for 'a fifty-dollar-a-day hotel suite' and other luxuries
Boss Finley showers on her. Before she ever appears on
stage, both Tom Junior and Heavenly tell their father that
they and everyone else in St Cloud know that Miss Lucy is
his mistress and has been even before the death of Mrs
Finley. And, to make matters worse, Tom Junior reveals
that Miss Lucy 'don't even talk good of you' (50). Exposing
Boss Finley's impotency in lipstick on the ladies' room
mirror of the hotel bar, she unintentionally causes him to
confront his waning sexual power. Like Del Lago and others
of Williams's heroines, she is 'an agent of truth forcing weak
men to face reality' (Clum, 140). In doing so, she exposes
herself to danger. Boss Finley retaliates with physical
violence, clamping a jewellery box on her finger.

Despite his violence, Miss Lucy is a survivor. When she
makes her entrance in Act Two, Scene Two, she is
described as '*dressed in a ball gown elaborately ruffled and very
bouffant like an antebellum Southern belle's. A single blonde curl is
arranged to switch girlishly at one side of her sharp little terrier face*'
(58). Like Scarlett O'Hara, to whom Chance compares her,
she holds on to her dignity and pride even under attack by

enemy forces and when scorned by her lover. But her
gentility and girlish behaviour is, Williams suggests, a
façade. Like a terrier, a dog used for hunting, she is quick
and wily. Miss Lucy wastes no time in retaliating. Seeing
someone new enter the bar, she immediately approaches
him, asking questions until she discovers that he is a heckler
'come to hear Boss Finley talk' (59). Providing the Heckler
with a jacket and tie and directing him to the ballroom
where the rally will take place, she seeks a revenge which
will expose Boss Finley's waning political potency.

Miss Lucy is one of the few characters who attempts to
help both Del Lago and Chance. Perhaps because she
prostituted herself to obtain a type of lifestyle similar to that
of Del Lago's – a lifestyle that Chance seeks and Del Lago is
potentially losing – Miss Lucy identifies with both of them.
When Miss Lucy, who has been trying to figure out what
has changed about Chance, ruffles his hair, he bristles. In
response, she says, 'Is your hair thinning? Maybe that's the
difference I noticed in your appearance'. Without intending
harm, she forces Chance to confront his failure when she
tells him in front of the crowd in the bar that Dan Hatcher
had seen him in Palm Beach working 'as a beach-boy at
some big hotel' (69). Even though she exposes his failure to
beat time and to be anything better than beach-boy, she
tries to save Chance from the monsters of St Cloud, urging
him to flee with her to New Orleans.

As the 'president of [Del Lago's] local fan club' (61), Miss
Lucy reveals that like Chance she bought into the
Hollywood dream, worshipping those whose names
appeared on the Silver Screen. When she sees Del Lago's
miserable state in Act Two, Scene Two, unlike Chance who
brushes her aside, Miss Lucy shows compassion: 'Honey, let
me fix that zipper for you. Hold still just a second. Honey,
let me take you upstairs. You mustn't be seen down here in
this condition' (76). Aware of how cruel the inhabitants of St
Cloud can be, Miss Lucy attempts to preserve Del Lago's
appearance, and by extension the Cinderella myth. While
she may not be able to assist her in much else, she tries to
make sure that Del Lago is presentable even in her

desperation – a skill that Miss Lucy has perfected. She shows no signs of distress though cut off financially from her former benefactor, Boss Finley.

Stage, film and television productions

Written in 1952 and first produced at the Studio M Playhouse in Coral Gables, Florida, in 1956, *Sweet Bird of Youth* underwent several revisions. The play did not make an impact on New York critics and audiences until March of 1959. The Broadway premiere took place at the Martin Beck Theatre and was directed by Elia Kazan who collaborated with Williams on *A Streetcar Named Desire*, *Camino Real* and *Cat on a Hot Tin Roof*. Jo Mielziner, also no stranger to Williams, designed the set and lighting. Paul Newman, who only a year before had starred in the film version of *Cat on a Hot Tin Roof*, was cast in the role of Chance Wayne and Geraldine Page was Alexandra Del Lago. *Sweet Bird of Youth* received mixed reviews from New York critics, many of whom felt Williams had gone too far. John J. O'Connor of *Audience* wrote,

> The play, a hodgepodge of familiar Williams themes, sensationalism, and pseudo-poetically stated truisms, might have been an interesting one-acter. Certainly its content and scope do not justify the two-and-a-half hour ordeal it now demands. (Quoted in Murphy, 160)

Moreover, the critic John Gassner reported that he 'was disturbed by the attempted focusing of sympathy on two self-confessed "monsters"' (123). Along with criticising Williams's sensationalism, Gassner, who overall praised the play, saw problems in the structure of *Sweet Bird of Youth*. He found the play weakened by 'the split dramatic construction that divides attention between the personal drama and an attack on racist demagoguery in the South' (123). Despite these reviews, the play is considered one of Williams's many successes. Audiences stood in long queues to see this play which ran for almost a year and a total of 375 performances. In addition to a positive audience reception, the play was nominated for four Tony Awards.

The Broadway revival of *Sweet Bird of Youth* at the
Harkness Theatre in 1975 also met with success. Gina
Mallet, a reviewer for *Time* magazine, wrote, 'Today [the
play] seems fatally misconceived, a sentimental melodrama
instead of a savage, black comedy on southern mores'.
Despite the problematic production, Irene Worth's
portrayal of Alexandra Del Lago was praised. Mallet and
other critics noted that Worth 'overwhelm[ed] the play,
with a sexy vibrato not unlike Al Jolson's, and stalk[ed] the
stage like a jaguar vacationing among field mice'. She won a
Tony for Best Actress.

Not until twenty-six years after its American debut did
the play reach London's West End. Directed by the Nobel
Prize-winning playwright Harold Pinter, the play opened at
the Haymarket Theatre on 8 July 1985. Despite the praise
Lauren Bacall received for her charming and cool portrayal
of Alexandra Del Lago, London critics and audiences were
disappointed. Mel Gussow, in his review of the London
production for the *New York Times*, argued that the play's
failure to captivate English audiences stemmed in part from
cultural expectations. He revealed that since its world debut,
English critics such as Kenneth Tynan have dismissed
Williams's work as 'operatic and hysterical'. Pinter's attempt
to create a cooler version of the play, however, diffused the
panic and anxiety of Chance Wayne and Alexandra Del
Lago, which ultimately for Gussow diminishes the angst of
Sweet Bird of Youth.

Nine years after the London debut of *Sweet Bird of Youth*,
the play was revived at the National Theatre. Directed by
Richard Eyre and starring Robert Knepper as Chance
Wayne and Clare Higgins as Alexandra Del Lago, this 1994
production restored the heated tension and anxiety absent
in Pinter's subdued production. According to critic Clara
Hieronymus of *The Tennessean*, while 'Williams's melodrama
ends up a sad spoof', London audiences 'listened attentively,
absorbed in its raffishly dramatic performance and gave it a
succession of curtain calls'. Indeed, most critics, while
acknowledging that the play is flawed and its themes are
perhaps no longer relevant, praised Eyre's production and

the acting of the two leads. Michael Billington of the
Guardian called Eyre's production 'superbly atmospheric'
with a 'knock-down performance from Clare Higgins as a
fading movie queen'. Knepper's performance, too, was
deemed exceptional. Neil Smith, in his article for *What's On*,
wrote, 'The role of Chance Wayne is an Everest for any
actor, but Knepper tackles the challenge head-on'. Michael
Coveney of *The Observer* called the production 'a blazing
restoration' and Dale Maitland Cartwright of the *Southern
Cross* decreed it 'A real stunner, make sure you see!'.

In 1962, the first film version of the play hit the big
screen, directed by Richard Brooks. Newman and Page
once again took on the roles of Chance and the Princess.
The film veers from the text in drastic ways and a dismayed
Williams complained that the happy ending to the film was
'a contradiction to the meaning of the play' (quoted in
Devlin, 275). However, the performances of Newman and
Page are unforgettable and Page won an Oscar for her part.
Despite the softening of the racial/political tensions, the
change from Heavenly Finley being infected with a venereal
disease to having an abortion and the film's happy ending,
which allowed Chance and Heavenly to unite after Tom
Junior breaks Chance's nose, the film's aura is definitely
Williams's, leaving the audience to wonder whether
Heavenly and Chance can really make it.

Nearly thirty years after the play hit the stage, the
American television broadcasting system NBC aired a new
version of *Sweet Bird of Youth* in 1989, directed by Nicholas
Roeg, starring Elizabeth Taylor as Alexandra Del Lago,
Mark Harmon as Chance Wayne and Rip Torn as Boss
Finley. Although in the fifties and sixties Taylor starred with
great success in film adaptations of plays, including the 1958
film adaptation of *Cat on a Hot Tin Roof* and the 1959 film
adaptation of *Suddenly Last Summer*, this made-for-television
version of the play is deeply disappointing. Despite restoring
the original ending (Chance's castration), this film is no
more faithful to the playtext than the earlier film;
production and acting leave much to be desired.

Further Reading

Selected works by Williams

The Theatre of Tennessee Williams, vol. 1: Battle of Angels, The Glass Menagerie, A Streetcar Named Desire, New York, New Directions, 1971

The Theatre of Tennessee Williams, vol. 2: The Eccentricities of a Nightingale, Summer and Smoke, The Rose Tattoo, Camino Real, New York, New Directions, 1976

The Theatre of Tennessee Williams, vol. 3: Cat on a Hot Tin Roof, Orpheus Descending, Suddenly Last Summer, New York: New Directions, 1971

The Theatre of Tennessee Williams, vol. 4: Sweet Bird of Youth, A Period of Adjustment, The Night of the Iguana, New York, New Directions, 1972

Cat on a Hot Tin Roof, with commentary and notes by Philip C. Kolin, London: Methuen Drama, 2010

The Glass Menagerie (with 'The Catastrophe of Success'), with commentary and notes by Stephen J. Bottoms, London: Methuen Drama, 2000

A Streetcar Named Desire, with commentary and notes by Patricia Hearn and Michael Hooper, London: Methuen Drama, 1984; reissued 2009

Five O'Clock Angel: Letters of Tennessee Williams to Maria St Just, ed. Alfred A. Knopf, New York: Knopf, 1990

Notebooks, ed. Margaret Bradham Thornton, New Haven and London: Yale University Press, 2006

Where I Live: Selected Essays, ed. Christine Day and Bob Woods, New York: New Directions, 1978

Full-length studies on Williams

Devlin, Albert J. (ed.), *Conversations with Tennessee Williams*, Jackson and London, University of Mississippi Press, 2000

Donahue, Francis, *The Dramatic World of Tennessee Williams*, New York: Frederick Ungar, 1964

Falk, Signi Lenea, *Tennessee Williams*, New York, Twayne, 1961

Griffin, Alice, *Understanding Tennessee Williams*, Columbia: University of South Carolina Press, 1995

Hayman, Robert, *Tennessee Williams: Everyone Else is an Audience*, New Haven: Yale University Press, 1993

Jackson, Esther Merle, *The Broken World of Tennessee Williams*, Madison: University of Wisconsin Press, 1965

Leverich, Lyle, *The Unknown Tennessee Williams*, New York: Norton, 1995

Murphy, Brenda, *Tennessee Williams and Elia Kazan: A Collaboration in the Theatre*, Cambridge, Cambridge University Press, 1992

Nelson, Benjamin, *Tennessee Williams: His Life and Work*, London: Peter Owen, 1961

Roudané, Matthew (ed.), *The Cambridge Companion to Tennessee Williams*, Cambridge: Cambridge University Press, 1997

Savran, David, *Communists, Cowboys and Queers: The Politics of Masculinity in the Work of Arthur Miller and Tennessee Williams*, Minneapolis: University of Minnesota Press, 1992

Smith-Howard, Alycia and Greta Heintzelman (eds), *Tennessee Williams: A Literary Reference to his Life and Work*, New York: Facts on File, 2005

Spoto, Donald, *The Kindness of Strangers: The Life of Tennessee Williams*, New York: Da Capo Press, 1997

Stanton, Stephen S. (ed.), *Tennessee Williams: A Collection of Critical Essays*, Englewood: Prentice Hall, 1977

Voss, Ralph F. (ed.), *Magical Muse: Millennial Essays on Tennessee Williams*, Tuscaloosa: University of Alabama Press, 2002

Wilmeth, Don and Christopher Bigsby (eds), *The Cambridge History of American Theatre: Vol. III: Post-World War II to the 1990s*, Cambridge: Cambridge University Press, 1998

Articles on *Sweet Bird of Youth*

Adler, Thomas, 'Monologues and Mirrors in *Sweet Bird of Youth*', in *Critical Essays on Tennessee Williams*, ed. Robert A. Martin, New York: G. K. Hall, 1997, pp. 143–51

Carrigan, Mary Ann, 'Memory, Dream, and Myth in the Plays of Tennessee Williams', in *Critical Essays on Tennessee Williams*, ed. Robert A. Martin, New York: G. K. Hall, 1997, pp. 221–33

Clum, John M., 'The Sacrificial Stud and the Fugitive Female in *Suddenly Last Summer, Orpheus Descending*, and *Sweet Bird of Youth*', in *The Cambridge Companion to Tennessee Williams*, ed. Matthew Roudané, Cambridge: Cambridge University Press, 1997, pp. 128–46

Debusscher, Gilbert, 'And the Sailor Turned into a Princess: New Light on the Genesis of *Sweet Bird of Youth*', *Studies in American Drama, 1945 to the Present*, 1 (1986), pp. 25–31

Di Giuseppe, Rita, 'Monsters: Tennessee Williams, Darwin and Freud', *Quaderni di Lingue e Letterature*, 16 (1991), pp. 163–73

Dukore, Bernard F., 'American Abelard: A Footnote to *Sweet Bird of Youth*', *College English*, 26.8 (1965), pp. 630–4

Gunn, Drewey Wayne, 'The Troubled Flight of Tennessee Williams's *Sweet Bird*: From Manuscript through Published Texts', *Modern Drama*, 24.1 (1981), pp. 26–35

Hays, Peter, 'Tennessee Williams's Use of Myth in *Sweet Bird of Youth*', *Educational Theatre Journal*, 18.3 (1966), pp. 255–8

Jackson, Ester M., 'Tennessee Williams: The Idea of a Plastic Form', in *Critical Essays on Tennessee Williams*, ed. Robert A. Martin, New York: G. K. Hall, 1997, pp. 191–208

Kolin, Philip C. (ed.), *American Playwrights since 1945: A Guide to Scholarship, Criticism, and Performance*, Westport: Greenwood Press, 1989

—, 'Parallels Between *Desire Under the Elms* and *Sweet Bird of Youth*', *Eugene O'Neill Review*, 13.2 (1989), pp. 23–35

Parker, Brian, 'Problems with Boss Finley', *Tennessee Williams Annual Review*, 9 (2007), pp. 53–65

Roulet, William M., '*Sweet Bird of Youth*: Williams's Redemptive Ethic', *Cithara*, 2 (1964), pp. 31–6

Schulte-Sassa, Linda, 'Fixing a Nation's Problems: When a *Sweet Bird of Youth* Crosses the Line', *Cultural Critique*, 43 (1999), pp. 13–37

Voss, Ralph F., 'Tennessee Williams's *Sweet Bird of Youth* and William Inge's *Bus Riley's Back in Town*: Coincidences from a Friendship', *American Drama*, 15.1 (2006), pp. 62–73

Theatre reviews

Bemrose, John, '*Sweet Bird of Youth*' (Royal Alexandra Theatre production), *MacLean's*, 2 May 1988

Corry, John, 'Broadway; Elizabeth Taylor's *Sweet Bird* is due in April', *New York Times*, 18 June 1982

Cropper, Martin, 'Unexpected Delights of Character and Charm' (Haymarket Theatre production), *The Times*, 10 July 1985

Gassner, John, 'Broadway in Review', *Educational Theatre Journal* 11, 2 (1959), pp. 117–26

Gussow, Mel, 'Critic's Notebook: The English Remain Cool to Tennessee Williams', *New York Times*, 1 August 1985

Hattersley, Roy, 'Endpiece Column', *Guardian*, 31 August 1985

Lahr, John, 'Fugitive Mind', *New Yorker*, 18 July 1994

Lewin, David, 'Bacall: The Need to Live Dangerously', *Courier Mail*, 20 July 1985

Lochte, Dick, '*Sweet Bird of Youth*' (Ahmanson Theatre production), *Los Angeles Magazine*, February 1987

Mallet, Gina, 'Petit Guignol', *Time*, 15 December 1975

Nightingale, Benedict, 'Off Season is High Season for Theater in London', *New York Times*, 11 August 1985

—, '*Sweet Bird of Youth*' (Haymarket Theatre production), *New Statesman*, 19 July 1985

O'Toole, Fintan, '*Sweet Bird of Youth*' (Liberty Hall, Dublin production), *Irish Times*, 5 September 2003

Selznick, Daniel, 'London Digs Deeper into Familiar Plays', *Christian Science Monitor*, 21 September 1994

'New Plays on Broadway' (Broadway premiere), *Time*, 23 March 1959

'The Poet of Obsession', *Harper's Bazaar*, April 1985

Film and television reviews

Brennan, Patricia, '*Sweet Bird of Youth*: Rip Torn Putting His Accent on the Bigot Boss' (NBC production), *Washington Post*, 1 October 1989

Carter, Alan, 'Tennessee Williams's *Sweet Bird of Youth*' (NBC production), *People Weekly*, 2 October 1989

Leonard, John, '*Sweet Bird of Youth*' (NBC production), *New York Times*, 2 October 1989

O'Connor, John J., 'Elizabeth Taylor's Star Turn as Williams's Aging Star' (NBC production), *New York Times*, 29 September 1989

Park, Jeannie, 'Playing *Sweet Bird of Youth*'s Abandoned Love, Cheryl Paris draws on her own unhappy past' (NBC production), *People Weekly*, 2 October 1989

'Putting on the Cat' (1962 film), *Time*, 30 March 1962

'*Sweet Bird of Youth*' (NBC production), *Variety*, 25 October 1989

Sweet Bird of Youth

Relentless caper for all those who step
The legend of their youth into the noon

Hart Crane

To Cheryl Crawford

Foreword
By Tennessee Williams

When I came to my writing desk on a recent morning, I found lying on my desk top an unmailed letter that I had written. I began reading it and found this sentence: 'We are all civilized people, which means that we are all savages at heart but observing a few amenities of civilized behavior.' Then I went on to say: 'I am afraid that I observe fewer of these amenities than you do. Reason? My back is to the wall and has been to the wall for so long that the pressure of my back on the wall has started to crumble the plaster that covers the bricks and mortar.'

Isn't it odd that I said the wall was giving way, not my back? I think so. Pursuing this course of free association, I suddenly remembered a dinner date I once had with a distinguished colleague. During the course of this dinner, rather close to the end of it, he broke a long, mournful silence by lifting to me his sympathetic gaze and saying to me, sweetly, 'Tennessee, don't you feel that you are blocked as a writer?'

I didn't stop to think of an answer; it came immediately off my tongue without any pause for planning. I said, 'Oh, yes, I've always been blocked as a writer but my desire to write has been so strong that it has always broken down the block and gone past it.'

Nothing untrue comes off the tongue that quickly. It is planned speeches that contain lies or dissimulations, not what you blurt out so spontaneously in one instant.

It was literally true. At the age of fourteen I discovered writing as an escape from a world of reality in which I felt acutely uncomfortable. It immediately became my place of retreat, my cave, my refuge. From what? From being called a sissy by the neighborhood kids, and Miss Nancy by my father, because I would rather read books in my grandfather's large and classical library than play marbles and baseball and other normal kid games, a result of a severe childhood illness and of excessive attachment to the female members of my family, who had coaxed me back into life.

I think no more than a week after I started writing I ran into the first block. It's hard to describe it in a way that will be understandable to anyone who is not a neurotic. I will try. All my life I have been haunted by the obsession that to desire a thing or to love a thing intensely is to place yourself in a vulnerable position, to be a possible, if not a probable, loser of what you most want. Let's leave it like that. That block has always been there and always will be, and my chance of getting, or achieving, anything that I long for will always be gravely reduced by the interminable existence of that block.

I described it once in a poem called 'The Marvelous Children.' 'He, the demon, set up barricades of gold and purple tinfoil, labeled Fear (and other august titles), which they, the children, would leap lightly over, always tossing backwards their wild laughter.'

But having, always, to contend with this adversary of fear, which was sometimes terror, gave me a certain tendency toward an atmosphere of hysteria and violence in my writing, an atmosphere that has existed in it since the beginning.

In my first published work, for which I received the big sum of thirty-five dollars, a story published in the July or August issue of *Weird Tales* in the year 1928, I drew upon a paragraph in the ancient histories of Herodotus to create a story of how the Egyptian queen, Nitocris, invited all of her enemies to a lavish banquet in a subterranean hall on the shores of the Nile, and how, at the height of this banquet, she excused herself from the table and opened sluice gates admitting the waters of the Nile into the locked banquet hall, drowning her unloved guests like so many rats.

I was sixteen when I wrote this story, but already a confirmed writer, having entered upon this vocation at the age of fourteen, and, if you're well acquainted with my writings since then, I don't have to tell you that it set the keynote for most of the work that has followed.

My first four plays, two of them performed in St. Louis, were correspondingly violent or more so. My first play professionally produced and aimed at Broadway was *Battle of Angels* and it was about as violent as you can get on the stage.

During the nineteen years since then I have only produced

five plays that are *not* violent: *The Glass Menagerie, You Touched Me, Summer and Smoke, The Rose Tattoo* and, recently in Florida, a serious comedy called *Period of Adjustment,* which is still being worked on.

What surprises me is the degree to which both critics and audience have accepted this barrage of violence. I think I was surprised, most of all, by the acceptance and praise of *Suddenly Last Summer.* When it was done off Broadway, I thought I would be critically tarred and feathered and ridden on a fence rail out of the New York theatre, with no future haven except in translation for theatres abroad, who might mistakenly construe my work as a castigation of American morals, not understanding that I write about violence in American life only because I am not so well acquainted with the society of other countries.

Last year I thought it might help me as a writer to undertake psychoanalysis and so I did. The analyst, being acquainted with my work and recognizing the psychic wounds expressed in it, asked me, soon after we started, 'Why are you so full of hate, anger and envy?'

Hate was the word I contested. After much discussion and argument, we decided that 'hate' was just a provisional term and that we would only use it till we had discovered the more precise term. But unfortunately I got restless and started hopping back and forth between the analyst's couch and some Caribbean beaches. I think before we called it quits I had persuaded the doctor that hate was not the right word, that there was some other thing, some other word for it, which we had not yet uncovered, and we left it like that.

Anger, oh yes! And envy, yes! But not hate. I think that hate is a thing, a feeling, that can only exist where there is no understanding. Significantly, good physicians never have it. They never hate their patients, no matter how hateful their patients may seem to be, with their relentless, maniacal concentration on their own tortured egos.

Since I am a member of the human race, when I attack its behavior toward fellow members I am obviously including myself in the attack, unless I regard myself as not human but superior to humanity. I don't. In fact, I can't expose a human weakness on the stage unless I know it through having it myself.

I have exposed a good many human weaknesses and brutalities and consequently I have them.

I don't even think that I am more conscious of mine than any of you are of yours. Guilt is universal. I mean a strong sense of guilt. If there exists any area in which a man can rise above his moral condition, imposed upon him at birth and long before birth, by the nature of his breed, then I think it is only a willingness to know it, to face its existence in him, and I think that at least below the conscious level, we all face it. Hence guilty feelings, and hence defiant aggressions, and hence the deep dark of despair that haunts our dreams, our creative work, and makes us distrust each other.

Enough of these philosophical abstractions, for now. To get back to writing for the theatre, if there is any truth in the Aristotelian idea that violence is purged by its poetic representation on a stage, then it may be that my cycle of violent plays have had a moral justification after all. I know that I have felt it. I have always felt a release from the sense of meaninglessness and death when a work of tragic intention has seemed to me to have achieved that intention, even if only approximately, nearly.

I would say that there is something much bigger in life and death than we have become aware of (or adequately recorded) in our living and dying. And, further, to compound this shameless romanticism, I would say that our serious theatre is a search for that something that is not yet successful but is still going on.

Synopsis of Scenes

Act One

Scene One   A bedroom in the Royal Palms Hotel, somewhere on the Gulf Coast.

Scene Two   The same. Later.

Act Two

Scene One   The terrace of Boss Finley's house in St Cloud.

Scene Two   The cocktail lounge and Palm Garden of the Royal Palms Hotel.

Act Three   The bedroom again.

Time

Modern, an Easter Sunday, from late morning till late night.

Setting and 'Special Effects'

The stage is backed by a cyclorama that should give a poetic unity of mood to the several specific settings. There are nonrealistic projections on this 'cyc', the most important and constant being a grove of royal palm trees. There is nearly always a wind among these very tall palm trees, sometimes loud, sometimes just a whisper, and sometimes it blends into a thematic music which will be identified, when it occurs, as 'The Lament'.

During the daytime scenes the cyclorama projection is a poetic abstraction of semitropical sea and sky in fair spring weather. At night it is the Palm Garden with its branches among the stars.

The specific settings should be treated as freely and sparingly as the sets for *Cat on a Hot Tin Roof* or *Summer and Smoke*. They'll be described as you come to them in the script.

Sweet Bird of Youth was presented at the Martin Beck Theatre in New York on 10 March 1959 by Cheryl Crawford. The cast was as follows:

Chance Wayne	Paul Newman
The Princess Kosmonopolis	Geraldine Page
Fly	Milton J. Williams
Maid	Patricia Ripley
George Scudder	Logan Ramsey
Hatcher	John Napier
Boss Finley	Sidney Blackmer
Tom Junior	Rip Torn
Aunt Nonnie	Martine Bartlett
Heavenly Finley	Diana Hyland
Charles	Earl Sydnor
Stuff	Bruce Dern
Miss Lucy	Madeleine Sherwood
The Heckler	Charles Tyner
Violet	Monica May
Edna	Hilda Brawner
Scotty	Charles McDaniel
Bud	Jim Jeter
Men in Bar	Duke Farley, Ron Harper, Kenneth Blake
Page	Glenn Stensel

Directed by Elia Kazan
Settings and lighting by Jo Mielziner
Costumes by Anna Hill Johnstone
Music by Paul Bowles

Act One

Scene One

A bedroom of an old-fashioned but still fashionable hotel somewhere along the Gulf Coast in a town called St Cloud. I think of it as resembling one of those 'Grand Hotels' around Sorrento or Monte Carlo, set in a Palm Garden. The style is vaguely 'Moorish'. The principal set-piece is a great double bed which should be raked toward the audience. In a sort of Moorish corner backed by shuttered windows is a wicker tabouret and two wicker stools, over which is suspended a Moorish lamp on a brass chain. The windows are floor length and they open out upon a gallery. There is also a practical door frame, opening onto a corridor: the walls are only suggested.

On the great bed are two figures, a sleeping woman, and a young man awake, sitting up, in the trousers of white silk pajamas. The sleeping woman's face is partly covered by an eyeless black satin domino to protect her from morning glare. She breathes and tosses on the bed as if in the grip of a nightmare. The young man is lighting his first cigarette of the day.

Outside the windows there is heard the soft, urgent cries of birds, the sound of their wings. Then a colored waiter, **Fly**, *appears at door on the corridor, bearing coffee-service for two. He knocks.* **Chance** *rises, pauses a moment at a mirror in the fourth wall to run a comb through his slightly thinning blond hair before he crosses to open the door.*

Chance   Aw, good, put it in there.

Fly   Yes, suh.

Chance   Give me the Bromo first. You better mix it for me, I'm –

Fly   Hands kind of shaky this mawnin'?

Chance (*shuddering after the Bromo*)   Open the shutters a little. Hey, I said a little, not much, not that much!

As the shutters are opened we see him clearly for the first time: he's in his late twenties and his face looks slightly older than that; you might describe

*it as a 'ravaged young face' and yet it is still exceptionally good-looking.
His body shows no decline, yet it's the kind of a body that white silk
pajamas are, or ought to be, made for. A church bell tolls, and from another
church, nearer, a choir starts singing the 'Hallelujah Chorus'. It draws
him to the window, and as he crosses, he says:*

I didn't know it was – Sunday.

Fly   Yes, suh, it's *Easter* Sunday.

Chance (*leans out a moment, hands gripping the shutters*)   Uh-
huh . . .

Fly   That's the Episcopal Church they're singin' in. The
bell's from the Catholic Church.

Chance   I'll put your tip on the check.

Fly   Thank you, Mr Wayne.

Chance (*as **Fly** starts for the door*)   Hey. How did you know my
name?

Fly   I waited tables in the Grand Ballroom when you used to
come to the dances on Saturday nights, with that real pretty
girl you used to dance so good with, Mr Boss Finley's daughter?

Chance   I'm increasing your tip to five dollars in return for a
favor, which is not to remember that you have recognized me
or anything else at all. Your name is Fly – shoo, Fly. Close the
door with no noise.

Voice Outside   Just a minute.

Chance   Who's that?

Voice Outside   George Scudder. (*Slight pause. **Fly** exits.*)

Chance   How did you know I was here?

George Scudder *enters: a coolly nice-looking, businesslike young
man who might be the head of the Junior Chamber of Commerce but is
actually a young doctor, about thirty-six or -seven.*

Scudder   The assistant manager that checked you in here last night phoned me this morning that you'd come back to St Cloud.

Chance   So you came right over to welcome me home?

Scudder   Your lady friend sounds like she's coming out of ether.

Chance   The Princess had a rough night.

Scudder   You've latched onto a Princess? (*Mockingly.*) Gee.

Chance   She's traveling incognito.

Scudder   Golly, I should think she would, if she's checking in hotels with *you*.

Chance   George, you're the only man I know that still says 'gee', 'golly', and 'gosh'.

Scudder   Well, I'm not the sophisticated type, Chance.

Chance   That's for sure. Want some coffee?

Scudder   Nope. Just came for a talk. A quick one.

Chance   Okay. Start talking, man.

Scudder   Why've you come back to St Cloud?

Chance   I've still got a mother and a girl in St Cloud. How's Heavenly, George?

Scudder   We'll get around to that later. (*He glances at his watch.*) I've got to be in surgery at the hospital in twenty-five minutes.

Chance   You operate now, do you?

Scudder (*opening doctor's bag*)   I'm Chief of Staff there now.

Chance   Man, you've got it made.

Scudder   Why have you come back?

Chance   I heard that my mother was sick.

Scudder   But you said, 'How's Heavenly,' not 'How's my mother,' Chance. (**Chance** *sips coffee.*) Your mother died a couple of weeks ago . . .

Chance *slowly turns his back on the man and crosses to the window. Shadows of birds sweep the blind. He lowers it a little before he turns back to* **Scudder**.

Chance   Why wasn't I notified?

Scudder   You were. A wire was sent you three days before she died at the last address she had for you, which was General Delivery, Los Angeles. We got no answer from that and another wire was sent you after she died, the same day of her death, and we got no response from that either. Here's the Church Record. The church took up a collection for her hospital and funeral expenses. She was buried nicely in your family plot and the church has also given her a very nice headstone. I'm giving you these details in spite of the fact that I know and everyone here in town knows that you had no interest in her, less than people who knew her only slightly, such as myself.

Chance   How did she go?

Scudder   She had a long illness, Chance. You know about that.

Chance   Yes. She was sick when I left here the last time.

Scudder   She was sick at heart as well as sick in her body at that time, Chance. But people were very good to her, especially people who knew her in church, and the Reverend Walker was with her at the end.

Chance *sits down on the bed. He puts out his unfinished cigarette and immediately lights another. His voice becomes thin and strained.*

Chance   She never had any luck.

Scudder   Luck? Well, that's all over with now. If you want to know anything more about that, you can get in touch with Reverend Walker about it, although I'm afraid he won't be likely to show much cordiality to you.

Chance   She's gone. Why talk about it?

Scudder   I hope you haven't forgotten the letter I wrote you soon after you last left town.

Chance   No. I got no letter.

Scudder   I wrote you in care of an address your mother gave me about a very important private matter.

Chance   I've been moving a lot.

Scudder   I didn't even mention names in the letter.

Chance   What was the letter about?

Scudder   Sit over here so I don't have to talk loud about this. Come over here. I can't talk loud about this. (**Scudder** *indicates the chair by the tabouret.* **Chance** *crosses and rests a foot on the chair.*) In this letter I just told you that a certain girl we know had to go through an awful experience, a tragic ordeal, because of past contact with you. I told you that I was only giving you this information so that you would know better than to come back to St Cloud, but you didn't know better.

Chance   I told you I got no letter. Don't tell me about a letter, I didn't get any letter.

Scudder   I'm telling you what I told you in this letter.

Chance   All right. Tell me what you told me, don't – don't talk to me like a club, a chamber of something. What did you tell me? What ordeal? What girl? Heavenly? Heavenly? George?

Scudder   I see it's not going to be possible to talk about this quietly and so I . . .

Chance (*rising to block* **Scudder**'s *way*)   Heavenly? What ordeal?

Scudder   We will not mention names. Chance, I rushed over here this morning as soon as I heard you were back in St Cloud, before the girl's father and brother could hear that you were back in St Cloud, to stop you from trying to get in touch with the girl and to get out of here. That is absolutely all I have to say to you in this room at this moment . . . But I hope I have said it in a way to impress you with the vital urgency of it, so you will leave . . .

Chance   Jesus! If something's happened to Heavenly, will you please tell me – what?

Scudder   I said no names. We are not alone in this room. Now when I go downstairs now, I'll speak to Dan Hatcher, assistant manager here . . . he told me you'd checked in here . . . and tell him you want to check out, so you'd better get Sleeping Beauty and yourself ready to travel, and I suggest that you keep on traveling till you've crossed the state line . . .

Chance   You're not going to leave this room till you've explained to me what you've been hinting at about my girl in St Cloud.

Scudder   There's a lot more to this which we feel ought not to be talked about to anyone, least of all to you, since you have turned into a criminal degenerate, the only right term for you, but, Chance, I think I ought to remind you that once long ago, the father of this girl wrote out a prescription for you, a sort of medical prescription, which is castration. You'd better think about that, that would deprive you of all you've got to get by on. (*He moves toward the steps.*)

Chance   I'm used to that threat. I'm not going to leave St Cloud without my girl.

Scudder (*on the steps*)   You don't have a girl in St Cloud. Heavenly and I are going to be married next month. (*He leaves abruptly.*)

Chance, *shaken by what he has heard, turns and picks up phone, and kneels on the floor.*

Chance   Hello? St Cloud 525. Hello, Aunt Nonnie? This is Chance, yes Chance. I'm staying at the Royal Palms and I . . . what's the matter, has something happened to Heavenly? Why can't you talk now? George Scudder was here and . . . Aunt Nonnie? Aunt Nonnie?

The other end hangs up. The sleeping woman suddenly cries out in her sleep. **Chance** *drops the phone on its cradle and runs to the bed.*

Chance (*bending over her as she struggles out of a nightmare*) Princess! Princess! Hey, *Princess Kos*! (*He removes her eyemask; she sits up gasping and staring wild-eyed about her.*)

Princess   Who are you? Help!

Chance (*on the bed*)   Hush now . . .

Princess   Oh . . . I . . . had . . . a *terrible* dream.

Chance   It's all right. Chance's with you.

Princess   Who?

Chance   Me.

Princess   I don't know who you are!

Chance   You'll remember soon, Princess.

Princess   I don't know, I don't know . . .

Chance   It'll come back to you soon. What are you reachin' for, honey?

Princess   Oxygen! Mask!

Chance   Why? Do you feel short-winded?

Princess   Yes! I have . . . air . . . shortage!

Chance (*looking for the correct piece of luggage*)   Which bag is your oxygen in? I can't remember which bag we packed it in. Aw, yeah, the crocodile case, the one with the combination lock. Wasn't the first number zero . . . (*He comes back to the bed, and reaches for a bag under its far side.*)

Princess (*as if with her dying breath*)   Zero, zero. Two zeros to the right and then back around to . . .

Chance   Zero, three zeros, two of them to the right and the last one to the left . . .

Princess   Hurry! I can't breathe, I'm dying!

Chance   I'm getting it, Princess.

Princess   HURRY!

Chance   Here we are, I've got it . . .

He has extracted from case a small oxygen cylinder and mask. He fits the inhalator over her nose and mouth. She falls back on the pillow. He places the other pillow under her head. After a moment, her panicky breath subsiding, she growls at him.

Princess   Why in hell did you lock it up in that case?

Chance (*standing at the head of the bed*)   You said to put all your valuables in that case.

Princess   I meant my jewelry, and you know it, you bastard!

Chance   Princess, I didn't think you'd have these attacks any more. I thought that having me with you to protect you would stop these attacks of panic, I . . .

Princess   Give me a pill.

Chance   Which pill?

Princess   A pink one, a pinkie, and vodka . . .

He puts the tank on the floor, and goes over to the trunk. The phone rings. **Chance** *gives the* **Princess** *a pill, picks up the vodka bottle and goes to the phone. He sits down with the bottle between his knees.*

Chance (*pouring a drink, phone held between shoulder and ear*) Hello? Oh, hello, Mr Hatcher – Oh? But Mr Hatcher, when we checked in here last night we weren't told that, and Miss Alexandra Del Lago . . .

Princess (*shouting*)   *Don't use my name!*

Chance   . . . is suffering from exhaustion, she's not at all well, Mr Hatcher, and certainly not in any condition to travel . . . I'm sure you don't want to take the responsibility for what might happen to Miss Del Lago . . .

Princess (*shouting again*)   *Don't use my name!*

Chance   . . . if she attempted to leave here today in the condition she's in . . . do you?

Princess   *Hang up!* (*He does. He comes over with his drink and the bottle to the* **Princess**.) I want to forget everything, I want to forget who I am . . .

Chance (*handing her the drink*)   He said that . . .

Princess (*drinking*)   Please shut up, I'm *forgetting*!

Chance (*taking the glass from her*)   Okay, go on, forget. There's nothing better than that, I wish I could do it . . .

Princess   I can, I will. I'm forgetting . . . I'm forgetting . . .

She lies down. **Chance** *moves to the foot of the bed, where he seems to be struck with an idea. He puts the bottle down on the floor, runs to the chaise and picks up a tape recorder. Taking it back to the bed, he places the recorder on the floor. As he plugs it in, he coughs.*

Princess   What's going on?

Chance   Looking for my toothbrush.

Princess (*throwing the oxygen mask on the bed*)   Will you please take that away.

Chance   Sure you've had enough of it?

Princess (*laughs breathlessly*)   Yes, for God's sake, take it away. I must look hideous in it.

Chance (*taking the mask*)   No, no, you just look exotic, like a princess from Mars or a big magnified insect.

Princess   Thank you, check the cylinder please.

Chance   For what?

Princess   Check the air left in it; there's a gauge on the cylinder that gives the pressure . . .

Chance   You're still breathing like a quarter horse that's been run a full mile. Are you sure you don't want a doctor?

Princess   No, for God's sake . . . no!

Chance   Why are you so scared of doctors?

Princess (*hoarsely, quickly*)   I don't need them. What happened is nothing at all. It happens frequently to me. Something disturbs me . . . adrenalin's pumped in my blood and I get short-winded, that's all, that's all there is to it . . . I woke up, I didn't know where I was or who I was with, I got panicky . . . adrenalin was released and I got short-winded . . .

Chance   Are you okay now, Princess? Huh? (*He kneels on the bed, and helps straighten up the pillows.*)

Princess   Not quite yet, but I will be. I will be.

Chance   You're full of complexes, plump lady.

Princess   What did you call me?

Chance   Plump lady.

Princess   Why do you call me that? Have I let go of my figure?

Chance   You put on a good deal of weight after that disappointment you had last month.

Princess (*hitting him with a small pillow*)   What disappointment? I don't remember any.

Chance   Can you control your memory like that?

Princess   Yes. I've had to learn to. What is this place, a hospital? And you, what are you, a male nurse?

Chance   I take care of you but I'm not your nurse.

Princess   But you're employed by me, aren't you? For some purpose or other?

Chance   I'm not on salary with you.

Princess   What are you on? Just expenses?

Chance   Yep. You're footing the bills.

Princess   I see. Yes, I see.

Chance   Why're you rubbing your eyes?

Princess   My vision's so cloudy! Don't I wear glasses, don't I have any glasses?

Chance   You had a little accident with your glasses.

Princess   What was that?

Chance   You fell on your face with them on.

Princess   Were they completely demolished?

Chance   One lens cracked.

Princess   Well, please give me the remnants. I don't mind waking up in an intimate situation with someone, but I like to see who it's with, so I can make whatever adjustment seems called for . . .

Chance (*rises and goes to the trunk, where he lights cigarette*)   You know what I look like.

Princess   No, I don't.

Chance   You did.

Princess   I tell you I don't remember, it's all gone away!

Chance   I don't believe in amnesia.

Princess   Neither do I. But you have to believe a thing that happens to you.

Chance   Where did I put your glasses?

Princess   Don't ask me. You say I fell on them. If I was in that condition I wouldn't be likely to know where anything is I had with me. What happened last night?

He has picked them up but not given them to her.

Chance   You knocked yourself out.

Princess   Did we sleep here together?

Chance   Yes, but I didn't molest you.

Princess   Should I thank you for that, or accuse you of cheating?

She laughs sadly.

Chance   I like you, you're a nice monster.

Princess   Your voice sounds young. Are you young?

Chance   My age is twenty-nine years.

Princess   That's young for anyone but an Arab. Are you very good-looking?

Chance   I used to be the best-looking boy in this town.

Princess   How large is the town?

Chance   Fair-sized.

Princess   Well, I like a good mystery novel, I read them to put me to sleep and if they don't put me to sleep, they're good; but this one's a little too good for comfort. I wish you would find me my glasses . . .

He reaches over headboard to hand the glasses to her. She puts them on and looks him over. Then she motions him to come nearer and touches his bare chest with her finger tips.

Well, I may have done better, but God knows I've done worse.

Chance   What are you doing now, Princess?

Princess   The tactile approach.

Chance   You do that like you were feeling a piece of goods to see if it was genuine silk or phony . . .

Princess   It feels like silk. Genuine! This much I do remember, that I like bodies to be hairless, silky-smooth gold!

Chance   Do I meet these requirements?

Princess   You seem to meet those requirements. But I still have a feeling that something is not satisfied in the relation between us.

Chance (*moving away from her*)   You've had your experiences, I've had mine. You can't expect everything to be settled at once . . . Two different experiences of two different people.

Naturally there's some things that have to be settled between them before there's any absolute agreement.

Princess (*throwing the glasses on the bed*)   Take that splintered lens out before it gets in my eye.

Chance (*obeying this instruction by knocking the glasses sharply on the bed table*)   You like to give orders, don't you?

Princess   It's something I seem to be used to.

Chance   How would you like to *take* them? To be a slave?

Princess   What time is it?

Chance   My watch is in hock somewhere. Why don't you look at yours?

Princess   Where's mine?

He reaches lazily over to the table, and hands it to her.

Chance   It's stopped, at five past seven.

Princess   Surely it's later than that, or earlier, that's no hour when I'm . . .

Chance   Platinum, is it?

Princess   No, it's only white gold. I never travel with anything very expensive.

Chance   Why? Do you get robbed much? Huh? Do you get 'rolled' often?

Princess   Get what?

Chance   'Rolled'. Isn't that expression in your vocabulary?

Princess   Give me the phone.

Chance   For what?

Princess   I said give me the phone.

Chance   I know. And I said for what?

Princess   I want to enquire where I am and who is with me.

Chance   Take it easy.

Princess   Will you give me the phone?

Chance   Relax. You're getting short-winded again . . . (*He takes hold of her shoulders.*)

Princess   Please let go of me.

Chance   Don't you feel secure with me? Lean back. Lean back against me.

Princess   Lean back?

Chance   This way, this way. There . . .

He pulls her into his arms. She rests in them, panting a little like a trapped rabbit.

Princess   It gives you an awful trapped feeling this, this memory block . . . I feel as if someone I loved had died lately, and I don't want to remember who it could be.

Chance   Do you remember your name?

Princess   Yes, I do.

Chance   What's your name?

Princess   I think there's some reason why I prefer not to tell you.

Chance   Well, I happen to know it. You registered under a phony name in Palm Beach but I discovered your real one. And you admitted it to me.

Princess   I'm the Princess Kosmonopolis.

Chance   Yes, and you used to be known as . . .

Princess (*sits up sharply*)   No, stop . . . will you let me do it? Quietly, in my own way? The last place I remember . . .

Chance   What's the last place you remember?

Princess   A town with the crazy name of Tallahassee.

Chance   Yeah. We drove through there. That's where I reminded you that today would be Sunday and we ought to lay in a supply of liquor to get us through it without us being dehydrated too severely, and so we stopped there but it was a college town and we had some trouble locating a package store, open . . .

Princess   But we did, did we?

Chance (*getting up for the bottle and pouring her a drink*)   Oh, sure, we bought three bottles of vodka. You curled up in the back seat with one of those bottles and when I looked back you were blotto. I intended to stay on the Old Spanish Trail straight through to Texas, where you had some oil wells to look at. I didn't stop here . . . I was stopped.

Princess   What by, a cop? Or . . .

Chance   No. No cop, but I was arrested by something.

Princess   My car. Where is my car?

Chance (*handing her the drink*)   In the hotel parking lot, Princess.

Princess   Oh, then, this is a hotel?

Chance   It's the elegant old Royal Palms Hotel in the town of St Cloud.

Gulls fly past window, shadows sweeping the blind: they cry out with soft urgency.

Princess   Those pigeons out there sound hoarse. They sound like gulls to me. Of course, they could be pigeons with laryngitis.

Chance *glances at her with his flickering smile and laughs softly.*

Princess   Will you help me please? I'm about to get up.

Chance   What do you want? I'll get it.

Princess   I want to go to the window.

Chance   What for?

Princess   To look out of it.

Chance   I can describe the view to you.

Princess   I'm not sure I'd trust your description. WELL?

Chance   Okay, *oopsa-daisy*.

Princess   My God! I said help me up, not . . . toss me onto the carpet! (*Sways dizzily a moment, clutching bed. Then draws a breath and crosses to the window.*)

Pauses as she gazes out, squinting into noon's brilliance.

Chance   Well, what do you see? Give me your description of the view, Princess?

Princess (*faces the audience*)   I see a palm garden.

Chance   And a four-lane highway just past it.

Princess (*squinting and shielding her eyes*)   Yes, I see that and a strip of beach with some bathers and then, an infinite stretch of nothing but water and . . . (*She cries out softly and turns away from the window.*)

Chance   What? . . .

Princess   Oh God, I remember the thing I wanted not to. The goddam end of my life! (*She draws a deep shuddering breath.*)

Chance (*running to her aid*)   What's the matter?

Princess   Help me back to bed. Oh God, no wonder I didn't want to remember, I was no fool!

He assists her to the bed. There is an unmistakable sympathy in his manner, however shallow.

Chance   Oxygen?

Princess (*draws another deep shuddering breath*)   No! Where's the stuff? Did you leave it in the car?

Chance   Oh, the stuff? Under the mattress. (*Moving to the other side of the bed, he pulls out a small pouch.*)

Princess   A stupid place to put it.

Chance (*sits at the foot of the bed*)   What's wrong with under the mattress?

Princess (*sits up on the edge of the bed*)   There's such a thing as chambermaids in the world, they make up beds, they come across lumps in a mattress.

Chance   This isn't pot. What is it?

Princess   Wouldn't that be pretty? A year in jail in one of those model prisons for distinguished addicts. What is it? Don't you know what it is, you beautiful, stupid young man? It's hashish, Moroccan, the finest.

Chance   Oh, hash! How'd you get it through customs when you came back for your comeback?

Princess   I didn't get it through customs. The ship's doctor gave me injections while this stuff was winging over the ocean to a shifty young gentleman who thought he could blackmail me for it. (*She puts on her slippers with a vigorous gesture.*)

Chance   Couldn't he?

Princess   Of course not. I called his bluff.

Chance   You took injections coming over?

Princess   With my neuritis? I had to. Come on, give it to me.

Chance   Don't you want it packed right?

Princess   You talk too much. You ask too many questions. I need something quick. (*She rises.*)

Chance   I'm a new hand at this.

Princess   I'm sure, or you wouldn't discuss it in a hotel room . . .

She turns to the audience, and intermittently changes the focus of her attention.

For years they all told me that it was ridiculous of me to feel that I couldn't go back to the screen or the stage as a middle-aged woman. They told me I was an artist, not just a star whose career depended on youth. But I knew in my heart that the legend of Alexandra Del Lago couldn't be separated from an appearance of youth . . .

There's no more valuable knowledge than knowing the right time to go. I knew it. I went at the right time to go. RETIRED! Where to? To what? To that dead planet the moon . . .

There's nowhere else to retire to when you retire from an art because, believe it or not, I really was once an artist. So I retired to the moon, but the atmosphere of the moon doesn't have any oxygen in it. I began to feel breathless, in that withered, withering country, of time coming after time not meant to come after, and so I discovered . . . Haven't you fixed it yet?

Chance *rises and goes to her with a cigarette he has been preparing.*

Princess   Discovered this!

And other practices like it, to put to sleep the tiger that raged in my nerves . . . Why the unsatisfied tiger? In the nerves jungle? Why is anything, anywhere, unsatisfied, and raging? . . .

Ask somebody's good doctor. But don't believe his answer because it isn't . . . the answer . . . if I had just been old but you see, I wasn't old . . .

I just wasn't young, not young, young. I just wasn't young any more . . .

Chance   Nobody's young any more . . .

Princess   But you see, I couldn't get old with that tiger still in me raging.

Chance   Nobody can get old . . .

Princess   Stars in retirement sometimes give acting lessons. Or take up painting, paint flowers on pots, or landscapes. I could have painted the landscape of the endless, withering country in which I wandered like a lost nomad. If I could paint deserts and nomads, if I could paint . . . hahaha . . .

Chance   Sh-sh-sh –

Princess   Sorry!

Chance   Smoke.

Princess   Yes, smoke! And then the young lovers . . .

Chance   Me?

Princess   You? Yes, finally you. But you come after the comeback. Ha . . . Ha . . . The glorious comeback, when I turned fool and came back . . . The screen's a very clear mirror. There's a thing called a close-up. The camera advances and you stand still and your head, your face, is caught in the frame of the picture with a light blazing on it and all your terrible history screams while you smile . . .

Chance   How do you know? Maybe it wasn't a failure, maybe you were just scared, just chicken, Princess . . . ha-ha-ha . . .

Princess   Not a failure . . . after that close-up they gasped . . . People gasped . . . I heard them whisper, their shocked whispers. Is that her? Is that her? Her? . . . I made the mistake of wearing a very elaborate gown to the *première*, a gown with a train that had to be gathered up as I rose from my seat and began the interminable retreat from the city of flames, up, up, up the unbearably long theatre aisle, gasping for breath and still clutching up the regal white train of my gown, all the way up the forever . . . length of the aisle, and behind me some small unknown man grabbing at me, saying, stay, stay! At last the top of the aisle, I turned and struck him, then let the train fall, forgot it, and tried to run down the marble stairs, tripped of course, fell and, rolled, rolled, like a sailor's drunk whore to the bottom . . . hands, merciful hands without faces, assisted me to get up. After that? Flight, just flight, not interrupted until I woke up this morning . . . Oh God it's gone out . . .

Chance   Let me fix you another. Huh? Shall I fix you another?

Princess   Let me finish yours. You can't retire with the out-crying heart of an artist still crying out, in your body, in your nerves, in your what? Heart? Oh, no that's gone, that's . . .

Chance (*he goes to her, takes the cigarette out of her hand and gives her a fresh one*)   Here, I've fixed you another one . . . Princess, I've fixed you another . . . (*He sits on the floor, leaning against the foot of the bed.*)

Princess   Well, sooner or later, at some point in your life, the thing that you lived for is lost or abandoned, and then . . . you die; or find something else. This is my something else . . . (*She approaches the bed.*) And ordinarily I take the most fantastic precautions against . . . detection . . . (*She sits on the bed, then lies down on her back, her head over the foot, near his.*) I cannot imagine what possessed me to let you know. Knowing so little about you as I seem to know.

Chance   I must've inspired a good deal of confidence in you.

Princess   If that's the case, I've gone crazy. Now tell me something. What is that body of water, that sea, out past the palm garden and four-lane highway? I ask you because I remember now that we turned west from the sea when we went onto that highway called the Old Spanish Trail.

Chance   We've come back to the sea.

Princess   What sea?

Chance   The Gulf.

Princess   The Gulf?

Chance   The Gulf of misunderstanding between me and you . . .

Princess   We don't understand each other? And lie here smoking this stuff?

Chance   Princess, don't forget that this stuff is yours, that you provided me with it.

Princess   What are you trying to prove? (*Church bells toll.*) Sundays go on a long time.

Chance   You don't deny it was yours.

Princess   What's mine?

Chance   You brought it into the country, you smuggled it through customs into the USA and you had a fair supply of it at that hotel in Palm Beach and were asked to check out before you were ready to do so, because its aroma drifted into the corridor one breezy night.

Princess   What are you trying to prove?

Chance   You don't deny that you introduced me to it?

Princess   Boy, I doubt very much that I have any vice that I'd need to introduce to you . . .

Chance   Don't call me 'boy'.

Princess   Why not?

Chance   It sounds condescending. And all my vices were caught from other people.

Princess   What are you trying to prove? My memory's come back now. Excessively clearly. It was this mutual practice that brought us together. When you came in my cabana to give me one of those papaya cream rubs, you sniffed, you grinned and said you'd like a stick too.

Chance   That's right. I knew the smell of it.

Princess   What are you trying to prove?

Chance   You asked me four or five times what I'm trying to prove, the answer is nothing. I'm just making sure that your memory's cleared up now. You do remember me coming in your cabana to give you those papaya cream rubs?

Princess   Of course I do, Carl!

Chance   My name is not Carl. It's Chance.

Princess   You called yourself Carl.

Chance   I always carry an extra name in my pocket.

Princess   You're not a criminal, are you?

Chance No ma'am, not me. You're the one that's committed a federal offense.

She stares at him a moment, and then goes to the door leading to the hall, looks out and listens.

What did you do that for?

Princess (*closing the door*) To see if someone was planted outside the door.

Chance You still don't trust me?

Princess Someone that gives me a false name?

Chance You registered under a phony one in Palm Beach.

Princess Yes, to avoid getting any reports or condolences on the disaster I ran from. (*She crosses to the window. There is a pause followed by 'The Lament'.*) And so we've not arrived at any agreement?

Chance No ma'am, not a complete one.

She turns her back to the window and gazes at him from there.

Princess What's the gimmick? The hitch?

Chance The usual one.

Princess What's that?

Chance Doesn't somebody always hold out for something?

Princess Are you holding out for something?

Chance Uh-huh . . .

Princess What?

Chance You said that you had a large block of stock, more than half ownership in a sort of a second-rate Hollywood studio, and could put me under contract. I doubted your word about that. You're not like any phony I've met before, but phonies come in all types and sizes. So I held out, even after we locked your cabana door for the papaya cream rubs . . . You wired for some contract papers we signed. It was notarized and witnessed by three strangers found in a bar.

Princess   Then why did you hold out, still?

Chance   I didn't have much faith in it. You know, you can buy those things for six bits in novelty stores. I've been conned and tricked too often to put much faith in anything that could still be phony.

Princess   You're wise. However, I have the impression that there's been a certain amount of intimacy between us.

Chance   A certain amount. No more. I wanted to hold your interest.

Princess   Well, you miscalculated. My interest always increases with satisfaction.

Chance   Then you're unusual in that respect, too.

Princess   In all respects I'm not common.

Chance   But I guess the contract we signed is full of loopholes?

Princess   Truthfully, yes, it is. I can get out of it if I wanted to. And so can the studio. Do you have any talent?

Chance   For what?

Princess   Acting, baby, ACTING!

Chance   I'm not as positive of it as I once was. I've had more chances than I could count on my fingers, and made the grade almost, but not quite, every time. Something always blocks me . . .

Princess   What? What? Do you *know*? (*He rises. 'The Lamentation' is heard very faintly.*) *Fear?*

Chance   No not fear, but terror . . . otherwise would I be your goddam caretaker, hauling you across the country? Picking you up when you fall? Well would I? Except for that block, by anything less than a star?

Princess   CARL!

Chance   Chance . . . Chance Wayne. You're stoned.

Princess   Chance, come back to your youth. Put off this false, ugly hardness and . . .

Chance   And be took in by every con-merchant I meet?

Princess   I'm not a phony, believe me.

Chance   Well, then, what is it you want? Come on say it, Princess.

Princess   Chance, come here. (*He smiles but doesn't move.*) Come here and let's comfort each other a little. (*He crouches by the bed; she encircles him with her bare arms.*)

Chance   Princess! Do you know something? All this conversation has been recorded on tape?

Princess   What are you talking about?

Chance   Listen. I'll play it back to you. (*He uncovers the tape recorder; approaches her with the earpiece.*)

Princess   How did you get that thing?

Chance   You bought it for me in Palm Beach. I said that I wanted it to improve my diction . . .

He presses the 'play' button on the recorder. The following in the left column can either be on a public address system, or can be cut.

Playback:

Princess   What is it? Don't you know what it is? You stupid, beautiful young man. It's hashish, Moroccan, the finest.

Chance   Oh, hash? How'd you get it through customs when you came back for your 'comeback'?

Princess   I didn't get it through customs. The ship's doctor . . .

Live:

Princess   What a smart cookie you are.

Chance   How does it feel to be over a great big barrel?

He snaps off the recorder and picks up the reels.

Princess   This is blackmail, is it? Where's my mink stole?

Chance   Not stolen.

He tosses it to her contemptuously from a chair.

Princess   Where is my jewel case?

Chance (*picks it up off the floor and throws it on the bed*)   Here.

Princess (*opens it up and starts to put on some jewelry*)   Every piece is insured and described in detail. Lloyd's in London.

Chance   *Who's* a smart cookie, Princess? You want your purse now so you can count your money?

Princess   I don't carry currency with me, just travelers' checks.

Chance   I noted that fact already. But I got a fountain pen you can sign them with.

Princess   Ho, ho!

Chance   'Ho, ho!' What an insincere laugh, if that's how you fake a laugh, no wonder you didn't make good in your comeback picture . . .

Princess   Are you serious about this attempt to blackmail me?

Chance   You'd better believe it. Your trade's turned dirt on you, Princess. You understand that language?

Princess   The language of the gutter is understood anywhere that anyone ever fell in it.

Chance   Aw, then you *do* understand.

Princess   And if I shouldn't comply with this order of yours?

Chance   You still got a name, you're still a personage, Princess. You wouldn't want *Confidential* or *Whisper* or *Hush-Hush* or the narcotics department of the FBI to get hold of one

of these tape-records, would you? And I'm going to make lots
of copies. Huh? Princess?

Princess   You are trembling and sweating . . . you see this
part doesn't suit you, you just don't play it well, Chance . . .
(**Chance** *puts the reels in a suitcase.*) I hate to think of what
kind of desperation has made you try to intimidate me, ME?
ALEXANDRA DEL LAGO? with that ridiculous threat. Why
it's so silly, it's touching, downright endearing, it makes me feel
close to you, Chance. You were well born, weren't you? Born
of good Southern stock, in a genteel tradition, with just one
disadvantage, a laurel wreath on your forehead, given too
early, without enough effort to earn it . . . where's your
scrapbook, Chance? (*He crosses to the bed, takes a travelers' checkbook
out of her purse, and extends it to her.*) Where's your book full of
little theatre notices and stills that show you in the background
of . . .

Chance   Here! Here! Start signing . . . or . . .

Princess (*pointing to the bathroom*)   Or WHAT? Go take a
shower under cold water. I don't like hot sweaty bodies in a
tropical climate. Oh, you, I do want and will accept, still . . .
under certain conditions which I will make very clear to you.

Chance   Here. (*Throws the checkbook toward the bed.*)

Princess   Put this away. And your leaky fountain pen . . .
When monster meets monster, one monster has to give way,
AND IT WILL NEVER BE ME. I'm an older hand at it . . .
with much more natural aptitude at it than you have . . . Now
then, you put the cart a little in front of the horse. Signed
checks are payment, delivery comes first. Certainly I can afford
it, I could deduct you, as my caretaker, Chance, remember
that I was a star before big taxes . . . and had a husband who
was a great merchant prince. He taught me to deal with
money . . . Now, Chance, please pay close attention while I tell
you the very special conditions under which I will keep you in
my employment . . . after this miscalculation . . .

Forget the legend that I was and the ruin of that legend.

Whether or not I do have a disease of the heart that places an early terminal date on my life, no mention of that, no reference to it ever. No mention of death, never, never a word on that odious subject. I've been accused of having a death wish but I think it's life that I wish for, terribly, shamelessly, on any terms whatsoever.

When I say now, the answer must not be later. I have only one way to forget these things I don't want to remember and that's through the act of love-making. That's the only dependable distraction so when I say now, because I need that distraction, it has to be now, not later.

She crosses to the bed. He rises from the opposite side of the bed and goes to the window. She gazes at his back as he looks out the window. Pause: 'The Lamentation'.

Princess (*finally, softly*)   Chance, I need that distraction. It's time for me to find out if you're able to give it to me. You mustn't hang onto your silly little idea that you can increase your value by turning away and looking out a window when somebody wants you . . . I want you . . . I say now and I mean now, then and not until then will I call downstairs and tell the hotel cashier that I'm sending a young man down with some travelers' checks to cash for me . . .

Chance (*turning slowly from the window*)   Aren't you ashamed, a little?

Princess   Of course I am. Aren't you?

Chance   More than a little . . .

Princess   Close the shutters, draw the curtain across them. (*He obeys these commands.*) Now get a little sweet music on the radio and come here to me and make me almost believe that we're a pair of young lovers without any shame.

Scene Two

As the curtain rises, the **Princess** *has a fountain pen in hand and is signing checks.* **Chance**, *now wearing dark slacks, socks and shoes of the fashionable loafer type, is putting on his shirt and speaks as the curtain opens.*

Chance   Keep on writing, has the pen gone dry?

Princess   I started at the back of the book where the big ones are.

Chance   Yes, but you stopped too soon.

Princess   All right, one more from the front of the book as a token of some satisfaction. I said some, not complete.

Chance (*picking up the phone*)   Operator – give me the cashier please.

Princess   What are you doing that for?

Chance   You have to tell the cashier you're sending me down with some travelers' checks to cash for you.

Princess   Have to? Did you say have to?

Chance   Cashier? Just a moment. The Princess Kosmonopolis. (*He thrusts the phone at her.*)

Princess (*into the phone*)   Who is this? But I don't want the cashier. My watch has stopped and I want to know the right time . . . five after three? Thank you . . . he says it's five after three. (*She hangs up and smiles at* **Chance**.) I'm not ready to be left alone in this room. Now let's not fight any more over little points like that, let's save our strength for the big ones. I'll have the checks cashed for you as soon as I've put on my face. I just don't want to be left alone in this place till I've put on the face that I face the world with, baby. Maybe after we get to know each other, we won't fight over little points any more, the struggle will stop, maybe we won't even fight over big points, baby. Will you open the shutters a little bit please? (*He doesn't seem to hear her. 'The Lament' is heard.*) I won't be able to see my face in the mirror . . . Open the shutters, I won't be able to see my face in the mirror.

Chance   Do you want to?

Princess (*pointing*)   Unfortunately I have to! Open the shutters! (*He does. He remains by the open shutters, looking out as 'The Lament' in the air continues.*)

Chance   – I was born in this town. I was born in St Cloud.

Princess   That's a good way to begin to tell your life story. Tell me your life story. I'm interested in it, I really would like to know it. Let's make it your audition, a sort of screen test for you. I can watch you in the mirror while I put my face on. And tell me your life story, and if you hold my attention with your life story, I'll know you have talent, I'll wire my studio on the Coast that I'm still alive and I'm on my way to the Coast with a young man named Chance Wayne that I think is cut out to be a great young star.

Chance (*moving out on the forestage*)   Here is the town I was born in, and lived in till ten years ago, in St Cloud. I was a twelve-pound baby, normal and healthy, but with some kind of quantity 'X' in my blood, a wish or a need to be different . . . The kids that I grew up with are mostly still here and what they call 'settled down', gone into business, married and bringing up children, the little crowd I was in with, that I used to be the star of, was the snob set, the ones with the big names and money. I didn't have either . . . (*The **Princess** utters a soft laugh in her dimmed-out area.*) What I had was . . . (*The **Princess** half turns, brush poised in a faint, dusty beam of light.*)

Princess   BEAUTY! Say it! Say it! What you had was beauty! I had it! I say it, with pride, no matter how sad, being gone, now.

Chance   Yes, well . . . the others . . . (*The **Princess** resumes brushing hair and the sudden cold beam of light on her goes out again.*) . . . are now members of the young social set here. The girls are young matrons, bridge-players, and the boys belong to the Junior Chamber of Commerce and some of them, clubs in

New Orleans such as Rex and Comus and ride on the Mardi
Gras floats. Wonderful? No, boring . . . I wanted, expected,
intended to get, something better . . . Yes, and I did, I got it. I
did things that fat-headed gang never dreamed of. Hell, when
they were still freshmen at Tulane or LSU or Ole Miss, I sang
in the chorus of the biggest show in New York, in *Oklahoma*,
and had pictures in *Life* in a cowboy outfit, tossin' a ten-gallon
hat in the air! YIP . . . EEEEEE! Ha-ha . . . And at the same
time pursued my other vocation . . . Maybe the only one I was
truly meant for, love-making . . . slept in the social register of
New York! Millionaires' widows and wives and debutante
daughters of such famous names as Vanderbrook and Masters
and Halloway and Connaught, names mentioned daily in
columns, whose credit cards are their faces . . . And . . .

Princess   What did they pay you?

Chance   I gave people more than I took. Middle-aged people
I gave back a feeling of youth. Lonely girls? Understanding,
appreciation! An absolutely convincing show of affection. Sad
people, lost people? Something light and uplifting! Eccentrics?
Tolerance, even odd things they long for . . . But always just at
the point when I might get something back that would solve
my own need, which was great, to rise to their level, the
memory of my girl would pull me back home to her . . . and
when I came home for those visits, man oh man how that town
buzzed with excitement. I'm telling you, it would blaze with it,
and then that thing in Korea came along. I was about to be
sucked into the Army so I went into the Navy, because a sailor's
uniform suited me better, the uniform was all that suited me,
though . . .

Princess   Ah-ha!

Chance (*mocking her*)   Ah-ha. I wasn't able to stand the
goddam routine, discipline . . . I kept thinking, this stops
everything. I was twenty-three, that was the peak of my youth
and I knew my youth wouldn't last long. By the time I got out,
Christ knows, I might be nearly thirty! Who would remember
Chance Wayne? In a life like mine, you just can't stop, you
know, can't take time out between steps, you've got to keep

going right on up from one thing to the other, once you drop out, it leaves you and goes on without you and you're washed up.

Princess I don't think I know what you're talking about.

Chance I'm talking about the parade. THE parade! The parade! The boys that go places, that's the parade I'm talking about, not a parade of swabbies on a wet deck. And so I ran my comb through my hair one morning and noticed that eight or ten hairs had come out, a warning signal of a future baldness. My hair was still thick. But would it be five years from now, or even three? When the war would be over, that scared me, that speculation. I started to have bad dreams. Nightmares and cold sweats at night, and I had palpitations, and on my leaves I got drunk and woke up in strange places with faces on the next pillow I had never seen before. My eyes had a wild look in them in the mirror . . . I got the idea I wouldn't live through the war, that I wouldn't come back, that all the excitement and glory of being Chance Wayne would go up in smoke at the moment of contact between my brain and a bit of hot steel that happened to be in the air at the same time and place that my head was . . . that thought didn't comfort me any. Imagine a whole lifetime of dreams and ambitions and hopes dissolving away in one instant, being blacked out like some arithmetic problem washed off a blackboard by a wet sponge, just by some little accident like a bullet, not even aimed at you but just shot off in space, and so I cracked up, my nerves did. I got a medical discharge out of the service and I came home in civvies, then it was when I noticed how different it was, the town and the people in it. Polite? Yes, but not cordial. No headlines in the papers, just an item that measured one inch at the bottom of page five saying that Chance Wayne, the son of Mrs Emily Wayne of North Front Street, had received an honorable discharge from the Navy as the result of illness and was home to recover . . . that was when Heavenly became more important to me than anything else . . .

Princess Is Heavenly a girl's name?

Chance   Heavenly is the name of my girl in St Cloud.

Princess   Is Heavenly why we stopped here?

Chance   What other reason for stopping here can you think of?

Princess   So . . . I'm being used. Why not? Even a dead racehorse is used to make glue. Is she pretty?

Chance (*handing* **Princess** *a snapshot*)   This is a flashlight photo I took of her, nude, one night on Diamond Key, which is a little sandbar about half a mile off shore which is under water at high tide. This was taken with the tide coming in. The water is just beginning to lap over her body like it desired her like I did and still do and will always, always. (**Chance** *takes back the snapshot.*) Heavenly was her name. You can see that it fits her. This was her at fifteen.

Princess   Did you have her that early?

Chance   I was just two years older, we had each other that early.

Princess   Sheer luck!

Chance   Princess, the great difference between people in this world is not between the rich and the poor or the good and the evil, the biggest of all differences in this world is between the ones that had or have pleasure in love and those that haven't and hadn't any pleasure in love, but just watched it with envy, sick envy. The spectators and the performers. I don't mean just ordinary pleasure or the kind you can buy, I mean great pleasure, and nothing that's happened to me or to Heavenly since can cancel out the many long nights without sleep when we gave each other such pleasure in love as very few people can look back on in their lives . . .

Princess   No question, go on with your story.

Chance   Each time I came back to St Cloud I had her love to come back to . . .

Princess   Something permanent in a world of change?

Chance   Yes, after each disappointment, each failure at something, I'd come back to her like going to a hospital . . .

Princess   She put cool bandages on your wounds? Why didn't you marry this Heavenly little physician?

Chance   Didn't I tell you that Heavenly is the daughter of Boss Finley, the biggest political wheel in this part of the country? Well, if I didn't I made a serious omission.

Princess   He disapproved?

Chance   He figured his daughter rated someone a hundred, a thousand per cent better than me, Chance Wayne . . . The last time I came back here, she phoned me from the drugstore and told me to swim out to Diamond Key, that she would meet me there. I waited a long time, till almost sunset, and the tide started coming in before I heard the put-put of an outboard motor boat coming out to the sandbar. The sun was behind her, I squinted. She had on a silky wet tank suit and fans of water and mist made rainbows about her . . . she stood up in the boat as if she was water-skiing, shouting things at me an' circling around the sandbar, around and around it!

Princess   She didn't come to the sandbar?

Chance   No, just circled around it, shouting things at me. I'd swim toward the boat, I would just about reach it and she'd race it away, throwing up misty rainbows, disappearing in rainbows and then circled back and shouting things at me again . . .

Princess   What things?

Chance   Things like, 'Chance, go away,' 'Don't come back to St Cloud.' 'Chance, you're a liar.' 'Chance, I'm sick of your lies!' 'My father's right about you!' 'Chance, you're no good any more.' 'Chance, stay away from St Cloud.' The last time around the sandbar she shouted nothing, just waved good-bye and turned the boat back to shore.

Princess   Is that the end of the story?

Chance   Princess, the end of the story is up to you. You want to help me?

Princess   I want to help you. Believe me, not everybody wants to hurt everybody. I don't want to hurt you, can you believe me?

Chance   I can if you prove it to me.

Princess   How can I prove it to you?

Chance   I have something in mind.

Princess   Yes, what?

Chance   Okay, I'll give you a quick outline of this project I have in mind. Soon as I've talked to my girl and shown her my contract, we go on, you and me. Not far, just to New Orleans, Princess. But no more hiding away, we check in at the Hotel Roosevelt there as Alexandra Del Lago and Chance Wayne. Right away the newspapers call you and give a press conference . . .

Princess   Oh?

Chance   Yes! The idea briefly, a local contest of talent to find a pair of young people to star as unknowns in a picture you're planning to make to show your faith in YOUTH, Princess. You stage this contest, you invite other judges, but your decision decides it!

Princess   And you and . . . ?

Chance   Yes, Heavenly and I win it. We get her out of St Cloud, we go to the West Coast together.

Princess   And me?

Chance   You?

Princess   Have you forgotten, for instance, that any public attention is what I least want in the world?

Chance   What better way can you think of to show the public that you're a person with bigger than personal interest?

Princess   Oh, yes, yes, but not true.

Chance   You could pretend it was true.

Princess   If I didn't despise pretending!

Chance   I understand. Time does it. Hardens people. Time and the world that you've lived in.

Princess   Which you want for yourself. Isn't that what you want? (*She looks at him then goes to the phone. Into phone.*) Cashier? Hello, Cashier? This is the Princess Kosmonopolis speaking. I'm sending down a young man to cash some travelers' checks for me. (*She hangs up.*)

Chance   And I want to borrow your Cadillac for a while . . .

Princess   What for, Chance?

Chance (*posturing*)   I'm pretentious. I want to be seen in your car on the streets of St Cloud. Drive all around town in it, blowing those long silver trumpets and dressed in the fine clothes you bought me . . . Can I?

Princess   Chance, you're a lost little boy that I really would like to help find himself.

Chance   I passed the screen test!

Princess   Come here, kiss me, I love you. (*She faces the audience.*) Did I say that? Did I mean it? (*Then to* **Chance** *with arms outstretched.*) What a child you are . . . Come here . . . (*He ducks under her arms, and escapes to the chair.*)

Chance   I want this big display. Big phony display in your Cadillac around town. And a wad a dough to flash in their faces and the fine clothes you've bought me, on me.

Princess   Did I buy you fine clothes?

Chance (*picking up his jacket from the chair*)   The finest. When you stopped being lonely because of my company at that Palm Beach hotel, you bought me the finest. That's the deal for tonight, to toot those silver horns and drive slowly around in the Cadillac convertible so everybody that thought I was washed up will see me. And I have taken my false or true contract to flash in the faces of various people that called me washed up. All right that's the deal. Tomorrow you'll get the car back and what's left of your money. Tonight's all that counts.

Princess   How do you know that as soon as you walk out of this room I won't call the police?

Chance   You wouldn't do that, Princess. (*He puts on his jacket.*) You'll find the car in back of the hotel parking lot, and the leftover dough will be in the glove compartment of the car.

Princess   Where will you be?

Chance   With my girl, or nowhere.

Princess   Chance Wayne! This was not necessary, all this. I'm not a phony and I wanted to be your friend.

Chance   Go back to sleep. As far as I know you're not a bad person, but you just got into bad company on this occasion.

Princess   I am your friend and I'm not a phony. (**Chance** *turns and goes to the steps.*) When will I see you?

Chance (*at the top of the steps*)   I don't know – maybe never.

Princess   Never is a long time, Chance, I'll wait.

She throws him a kiss.

Chance   So long.

The **Princess** *stands looking after him as the lights dim and the curtain closes.*

Act Two

Scene One

The terrace of **Boss Finley**'s *house, which is a frame house of Victorian Gothic design, suggested by a doorframe at the right and a single white column. As in the other scenes, there are no walls, the action occurring against the sky and sea cyclorama.*

The Gulf is suggested by the brightness and the gulls crying as in Act One. There is only essential porch furniture, Victorian wicker but painted bone white. The men should also be wearing white or off-white suits: the tableau is all blue and white, as strict as a canvas of Georgia O'Keeffe's.

At the rise of the curtain, **Boss Finley** *is standing in the center and* **George Scudder** *nearby.*

Boss Finley   Chance Wayne had my daughter when she was fifteen.

Scudder   That young . . .

Boss   When she was fifteen he had her. Know how I know? Some flashlight photos were made of her, naked, on Diamond Key.

Scudder   By Chance Wayne?

Boss   My little girl was fifteen, barely out of her childhood when – (*Calling offstage.*) Charles –

Charles enters.

Boss   Call Miss Heavenly –

Charles (*concurrently*)   Miss Heavenly. Miss Heavenly. Your daddy wants to see you.

Charles leaves.

Boss (*to* **Scudder**)   By Chance Wayne? Who the hell else do you reckon? I seen them. He had them developed by some studio in Pass Christian that made more copies of them than

Chance Wayne ordered and these photos were circulated.
I seen them. That was when I first warned the son of a bitch
to git and out of St Cloud. But he's back in St Cloud right
now. I tell you –

Scudder   Boss, let me make a suggestion. Call off this rally,
I mean your appearance at it, and take it easy tonight. Go out
on your boat, you and Heavenly take a short cruise on *The
Starfish* . . .

Boss   I'm not about to start sparing myself. Oh, I know, I'll
have me a coronary and go like that. But not because Chance
Wayne had the unbelievable gall to come back to St Cloud.
(*Calling offstage.*) Tom Junior!

Tom Junior (*offstage*)   Yes, sir!

Boss   Has he checked out yet?

Tom Junior (*entering*)   Hatcher says he called their room at
the Royal Palms, and Chance Wayne answered the phone, and
Hatcher says . . .

Boss   Hatcher says – who's Hatcher?

Tom Junior   Dan Hatcher.

Boss   I hate to expose my ignorance like this but the name
Dan Hatcher has no more meaning to me than the name of
Hatcher, which is none whatsoever.

Scudder (*quietly, deferentially*)   Hatcher, Dan Hatcher, is the
assistant manager of the Royal Palms Hotel, and the man that
informed me this morning that Chance Wayne was back in St
Cloud.

Boss   Is this Hatcher a talker, or can he keep his mouth
shut?

Scudder   I think I impressed him how important it is to
handle this thing discreetly.

Boss   Discreetly, like you handled that operation you done
on my daughter, so discreetly that a hillbilly heckler is shouting
me questions about it wherever I speak?

Scudder   I went to fantastic lengths to preserve the secrecy of that operation.

Tom Junior   When Papa's upset he hits out at anyone near him.

Boss   I just want to know – has Wayne left?

Tom Junior   Hatcher says that Chance Wayne told him that this old movie star that he's latched onto . . .

Scudder   Alexandra Del Lago.

Tom Junior   She's not well enough to travel.

Boss   Okay, you're a doctor, remove her to a hospital. Call an ambulance and haul her out of the Royal Palms Hotel.

Scudder   Without her consent?

Boss   Say she's got something contagious, typhoid, bubonic plague. Haul her out and slap a quarantine on her hospital door. That way you can separate them. We can remove Chance Wayne from St Cloud as soon as this Miss Del Lago is removed from Chance Wayne.

Scudder   I'm not so sure that's the right way to go about it.

Boss   Okay, you think of a way. My daughter's no whore, but she had a whore's operation after the last time he had her. I don't want him passin' another night in St Cloud. Tom Junior.

Tom Junior   Yes, sir.

Boss   I want him gone by tomorrow – tomorrow commences at midnight.

Tom Junior   I know what to do, Papa. Can I use the boat?

Boss   Don't ask me, don't tell me nothin' –

Tom Junior   Can I have *The Starfish* tonight?

Boss   I don't want to know how, just go about it. Where's your sister?

Charles *appears on the gallery, points out* **Heavenly** *lying on the beach to* **Boss** *and exits.*

Tom Junior   She's lyin' out on the beach like a dead body washed up on it.

Boss (*calling*)   Heavenly!

Tom Junior   Gawge, I want you with me on this boat trip tonight, Gawge.

Boss (*calling*)   Heavenly!

Scudder   I know what you mean, Tom Junior, but I couldn't be involved in it. I can't even know about it.

Boss (*calling again*)   Heavenly!

Tom Junior   Okay, don't be involved in it. There's a pretty fair doctor that lost his license for helping a girl out of trouble, and he won't be so goddam finicky about doing this absolutely just thing.

Scudder   I don't question the moral justification, which is complete without question . . .

Tom Junior   Yeah, complete without question.

Scudder   But I am a reputable doctor, I haven't lost my license. I'm chief of staff at the great hospital put up by your father . . .

Tom Junior   I said, don't know about it.

Scudder   No, sir, I won't know about it . . . (**Boss** *starts to cough.*) I can't afford to, and neither can your father . . . (**Scudder** *goes to gallery writing prescription.*)

Boss   Heavenly! Come up here, sugar. (*To* **Scudder**.) What's that you're writing?

Scudder   Prescription for that cough.

Boss   Tear it up, throw it away. I've hawked and spit all my life, and I'll be hawking and spitting in the hereafter. You all can count on that.

Auto horn is heard.

Tom Junior (*leaps up on the gallery and starts to leave*)   Papa, he's drivin' back by.

Boss   Tom Junior. (**Tom Junior** *stops.*)

Tom Junior   Is Chance Wayne insane?

Scudder   Is a criminal degenerate sane or insane is a question that lots of law courts haven't been able to settle.

Boss   Take it to the Supreme Court, they'll hand you down a decision on that question. They'll tell you a handsome young criminal degenerate like Chance Wayne is the mental and moral equal of any white man in the country.

Tom Junior   He's stopped at the foot of the drive.

Boss   Don't move, don't move, Tom Junior.

Tom Junior   I'm not movin', Papa.

Chance (*offstage*)   Aunt Nonnie! Hey, Aunt Nonnie!

Boss   What's he shouting?

Tom Junior   He's shouting at Aunt Nonnie.

Boss   Where is she?

Tom Junior   Runnin' up the drive like a dog-track rabbit.

Boss   He ain't followin', is he?

Tom Junior   Nope. He's drove away.

Aunt Nonnie *appears before the veranda, terribly flustered, rooting in her purse for something, apparently blind to the men on the veranda.*

Boss   Whatcha lookin' for, Nonnie?

Nonnie (*stopping short*)   Oh – I didn't notice you, Tom. I was looking for my *door* key.

Boss   Door's open, Nonnie, it's wide open, like a church door.

Nonnie (*laughing*)   Oh, ha, ha . . .

Boss   Why didn't you answer that good-lookin' boy in the Cadillac car that shouted at you, Nonnie?

Nonnie   Oh. I hoped you hadn't seen him. (*Draws a deep breath and comes onto the terrace, closing her white purse.*) That was Chance Wayne. He's back in St Cloud, he's at the Royal Palms, he's –

Boss   Why did you snub him like that? After all these years of devotion?

Nonnie   I went to the Royal Palms to warn him not to stay here but –

Boss   He was out showing off in that big white Cadillac with the trumpet horns on it.

Nonnie   I left a message for him, I –

Tom Junior   What was the message, Aunt Nonnie? Love and kisses?

Nonnie   Just get out of St Cloud right away, Chance.

Tom Junior   He's gonna git out, but not in that fishtail Caddy.

Nonnie (*to* **Tom Junior**)   I hope you don't mean violence – (*Turning to* **Boss**.) Does he, Tom? Violence don't solve problems. It never solves young people's problems. If you will leave it to me, I'll get him out of St Cloud. I can, I will, I promise. I don't think Heavenly knows he's back in St Cloud. Tom, you know, Heavenly says it wasn't Chance that – she says it wasn't Chance.

Boss   You're like your dead sister, Nonnie, gullible as my wife was. You don't know a lie if you bump into it on a street in the daytime. Now go out there and tell Heavenly I want to see her.

Nonnie   Tom, she's not well enough to –

Boss   Nonnie, you got a whole lot to answer for.

Nonnie   Have I?

Boss   Yes, you sure have, Nonnie. You favored Chance Wayne, encouraged, aided and abetted him in his corruption

of Heavenly over a long, long time. You go get her. You sure
do have a lot to answer for. You got a helluva lot to answer for.

Nonnie   I remember when Chance was the finest, nicest,
sweetest boy in St Cloud, and he stayed that way till you, till
you –

Boss   Go get her, go get her! (*She leaves by the far side of the
terrace. After a moment her voice is heard calling, 'Heavenly? Heavenly?'*)
It's a curious thing, a mighty peculiar thing, how often a man
that rises to high public office is drug back down by every soul
he harbors under his roof. He harbors them under his roof,
and they pull the roof down on him. Every last living one of
them.

Tom Junior   Does that include me, Papa?

Boss   If the shoe fits, put it on you.

Tom Junior   How does that shoe fit me?

Boss   If it pinches your foot, just slit it down the sides a little
– it'll feel comfortable on you.

Tom Junior   Papa, you are UNJUST.

Boss   What do you want credit for?

Tom Junior   I have devoted the past year to organizin' the
'Youth for Tom Finley' clubs.

Boss   I'm carryin' Tom Finley Junior on my ticket.

Tom Junior   You're lucky to have me on it.

Boss   How do you figure I'm lucky to have you on it?

Tom Junior   I got more newspaper coverage in the last six
months than . . .

Boss   Once for drunk drivin', once for a stag party you
thrown in Capitol City that cost me five thousand dollars to
hush it up!

Tom Junior   You are so unjust, it . . .

Boss   And everyone knows you had to be drove through school like a blazeface mule pullin' a plow uphill: flunked out of college with grades that only a moron would have an excuse for.

Tom Junior   I got readmitted to college.

Boss   At my insistence. By fake examinations, answers provided beforehand, stuck in your fancy pockets. And your promiscuity. Why, these Youth for Tom Finley clubs are practically nothin' but gangs of juvenile delinquents, wearin' badges with my name and my photograph on them.

Tom Junior   How about your well-known promiscuity, Papa? How about your Miss Lucy?

Boss   Who is Miss Lucy?

Tom Junior (*laughing so hard he staggers*)   Who is Miss Lucy? You don't even know who she is, this woman you keep in a fifty-dollar-a-day hotel suite at the Royal Palms, Papa?

Boss   What're you talkin' about?

Tom Junior   That rides down the Gulf Stream Highway with a motorcycle escort blowin' their sirens like the Queen of Sheba was going into New Orleans for the day. To use her charge accounts there. And you ask who's Miss Lucy? She don't even talk good of you. She says you're too old for a lover.

Boss   That is a goddam lie. Who says Miss Lucy says that?

Tom Junior   She wrote it with lipstick on the ladies' room mirror at the Royal Palms.

Boss   Wrote what?

Tom Junior   I'll quote it to you exactly. 'Boss Finley,' she wrote, 'is too old to cut the mustard.'

Pause: the two stags, the old and the young one, face each other, panting. **Scudder** *has discreetly withdrawn to a far end of porch.*

Boss   I don't believe this story!

Tom Junior   Don't believe it.

Boss   I will check on it, however.

Tom Junior   I already checked on it. Papa, why don't you get rid of her, huh, Papa?

Boss Finley *turns away, wounded, baffled: stares out at the audience with his old, bloodshot eyes as if he thought that someone out there had shouted a question at him which he didn't quite hear.*

Boss   Mind your own goddam business. A man with a mission, which he holds sacred, and on the strength of which he rises to high public office – crucified in this way, publicly, by his own offspring.

Heavenly *has entered on the gallery.*

Boss   Ah, here she is, here's my little girl. (*Stopping* **Heavenly**.) You stay here, honey. I think you all had better leave me alone with Heavenly now, huh-yeah . . . (**Tom Junior** *and* **Scudder** *exit.*) Now, honey, you stay here. I want to have a talk with you.

Heavenly   Papa, I can't talk now.

Boss   It's necessary.

Heavenly   I can't, I can't talk now.

Boss   All right, don't talk, just listen.

But she doesn't want to listen, starts away. He would have restrained her forcibly if an old colored manservant, **Charles**, *had not, at that moment, come out on the porch. He carries a stick, a hat, a package, wrapped as a present. Puts them on a table.*

Charles   It's five o'clock, Mister Finley.

Boss   Huh? Oh – thanks . . .

Charles *turns on a coach lamp by the door. This marks a formal division in the scene. The light change is not realistic; the light doesn't seem to come from the coach lamp but from a spectral radiance in the sky, flooding the terrace.*

The sea wind sings. **Heavenly** *lifts her face to it. Later that night may be stormy, but now there is just a quickness and freshness coming in from the Gulf.* **Heavenly** *is always looking that way, toward the Gulf, so* *that the light from Point Lookout catches her face with its repeated soft stroke of clarity.*

In her father, a sudden dignity is revived. Looking at his very beautiful daughter, he becomes almost stately. He approaches her, soon as the colored man returns inside, like an aged courtier comes deferentially up to a crown princess or infanta. It's important not to think of his attitude toward her in the terms of crudely conscious incestuous feeling, but just in the natural terms of almost any aging father's feeling for a beautiful young daughter who reminds him of a dead wife that he desired intensely when she was the age of his daughter.

At this point there might be a phrase of stately, Mozartian music, suggesting a court dance. The flagged terrace may suggest the parquet floor of a ballroom and the two players' movements may suggest the stately, formal movements of a court dance of that time; but if this effect is used, it should be just a suggestion. The change toward 'stylization' ought to be held in check.

Boss   You're still a beautiful girl.

Heavenly   Am I, Papa?

Boss   Of course you are. Lookin' at you nobody could guess that –

Heavenly (*laughs*)   The embalmers must have done a good job on me, Papa . . .

Boss   You got to quit talkin' like that. (*Then, seeing* **Charles**.) Will you get back in the house! (*Phone rings.*)

Charles   Yes, sir, I was just –

Boss   Go on in! If that phone call is for me, I'm in only to the governor of the state and the president of the Tidewater Oil Corporation.

Charles (*offstage*)   It's for Miss Heavenly again.

Boss   Say she ain't in.

Charles   Sorry, she ain't in.

Heavenly *has moved upstage to the low parapet or sea wall that separates the courtyard and lawn from the beach. It is early dusk. The coach lamp has cast a strange light on the setting, which is neoromantic.* **Heavenly** *stops by an ornamental urn containing a tall fern that the salty Gulf wind has stripped nearly bare. The* **Boss** *follows her, baffled.*

Boss   Honey, you say and do things in the presence of people as if you had no regard of the fact that people have ears to hear you and tongues to repeat what they hear. And so you become a issue.

Heavenly   Become what, Papa?

Boss   A issue, a issue, subject of talk, of scandal – which can defeat the mission that –

Heavenly   Don't give me your Voice of God speech. Papa, there was a time when you could have saved me, by letting me marry a boy that was still young and clean, but instead you drove him away, drove him out of St Cloud. And when he came back, you took me out of St Cloud, and tried to force me to marry a fifty-year-old money bag that you wanted something out of –

Boss   Now, honey –

Heavenly   – and then another, another, all of them ones that you wanted something out of. I'd gone, so Chance went away. Tried to compete, make himself big as these big shots you wanted to use me for a bond with. He went. He tried. The right doors wouldn't open, and so he went in the wrong ones, and – Papa, you married for love, why wouldn't you let me do it, while I was alive, inside, and the boy still clean, still decent?

Boss   Are you reproaching me for – ?

Heavenly (*shouting*)   Yes, I am, Papa, I am. You married for love, but you wouldn't let me do it, and even though you'd done it, you broke Mama's heart, Miss Lucy had been your mistress –

Boss   Who is Miss Lucy?

Heavenly   Oh, Papa, she was your mistress long before
Mama died. And Mama was just a front for you. Can I go in
now, Papa? Can I go in now?

Boss   No, no, not till I'm through with you. What a terrible,
terrible thing for my baby to say . . . (*He takes her in his arms.*)
Tomorrow, tomorrow morning, when the big after-Easter sales
commence in the stores – I'm gonna send you in town with a
motorcycle escort, straight to the Maison Blanche. When you
arrive at the store, I want you to go directly up to the office of
Mr Harvey C. Petrie and tell him to give you unlimited credit
there. Then go down and outfit yourself as if you was – buyin'
a trousseau to marry the Prince of Monaco . . . Purchase a full
wardrobe, includin' furs. Keep 'em in storage until winter.
Gown? Three, four, five, the most lavish. Slippers? Hell, pairs
and pairs of 'em. Not one hat – but a dozen. I made a pile of
dough on a deal involvin' the sale of rights to oil under water
here lately, and baby, I want you to buy a piece of jewelry.
Now about that, you better tell Harvey to call me. Or better
still, maybe Miss Lucy had better help you select it. She's wise
as a backhouse rat when it comes to a stone, that's for sure . . .
Now where'd I buy that clip that I give your mama? D'you
remember the clip I bought your mama? Last thing I give your
mama before she died . . . I knowed she was dyin' when I bought
her that clip, and I bought that clip for fifteen thousand dollars
mainly to make her think she was going to get well . . . When I
pinned it on her on the nightgown she was wearing, that poor
thing started crying. She said, for God's sake, Boss, what does
a dying woman want with such a big diamond? I said to her,
honey, look at the price tag on it. What does the price tag say?
See them five figures, that one and that five and them three
noughts on there? Now, honey, make sense, I told her. If you
was dying, if there was any chance of it, would I invest fifteen
grand in a diamond clip to pin on the neck of a shroud? Ha,
haha. That made the old lady laugh. And she sat up as bright
as a little bird in that bed with the diamond clip on, receiving
callers all day, and laughing and chatting with them, with that
diamond clip on inside and she died before midnight, with that
diamond clip on her. And not till the very last minute did she

believe that the diamonds wasn't a proof that she wasn't dying. (*He moves to terrace, takes off robe and starts to put on tuxedo coat.*)

Heavenly   Did you bury her with it?

Boss   Bury her with it? Hell, no. I took it back to the jewelry store in the morning.

Heavenly   Then it didn't cost you fifteen grand after all.

Boss   Hell, did I care what it cost me? I'm not a small man. I wouldn't have cared one hoot if it cost me a million . . . if at that time I had that kind of loot in my pockets. It would have been worth that money to see that one little smile your mama bird give me at noon of the day she was dying.

Heavenly   I guess that shows, demonstrates very clearly, that you have got a pretty big heart after all.

Boss   Who doubts it then? Who? Who ever? (*He laughs.*)

Heavenly *starts to laugh and then screams hysterically. She starts going toward the house.* **Boss** *throws down his cane and grabs her.*

Boss   Just a minute, Missy. Stop it. Stop it. Listen to me, I'm gonna tell you something. Last week in New Bethesda, when I was speaking on the threat of desegregation to white women's chastity in the South, some heckler in the crowd shouted out, 'Hey, Boss Finley, how about your daughter? How about that operation you had done on your daughter at the Thomas J. Finley hospital in St Cloud? Did she put on black in mourning for her appendix?' Same heckler, same question when I spoke in the Coliseum at the state capital.

Heavenly   What was your answer to him?

Boss   He was removed from the hall at both places and roughed up a little outside it.

Heavenly   Papa, you have got an illusion of power.

Boss   I have power, which is not an illusion.

Heavenly   Papa, I'm sorry my operation has brought this embarrassment on you, but can you imagine it, Papa? I felt worse than embarrassed when I found out that Dr George Scudder's knife had cut the youth out of my body, made me an old childless woman. Dry, cold, empty, like an old woman. I feel as if I ought to rattle like a dead dried-up vine when the Gulf wind blows, but, Papa – I won't embarrass you any more. I've made up my mind about something. If they'll let me, accept me, I'm going into a convent.

Boss (*shouting*)   You ain't going into no convent. This state is a Protestant region and a daughter in a convent would politically ruin me. Oh, I know, you took your mama's religion because in your heart you always wished to defy me. Now, tonight, I'm addressing the Youth for Tom Finley clubs in the ballroom of the Royal Palms Hotel. My speech is going out over a national TV network, and Missy, you're going to march in the ballroom on my arm. You're going to be wearing the stainless white of a virgin, with a Youth for Tom Finley button on one shoulder and a corsage of lilies on the other. You're going to be on the speaker's platform with me, you on one side of me and Tom Junior on the other, to scotch these rumors about your corruption. And you're gonna wear a proud happy smile on your face, you're gonna stare straight out at the crowd in the ballroom with pride and joy in your eyes. Lookin' at you, all in white like a virgin, nobody would dare to speak or believe the ugly stories about you. I'm relying a great deal on this campaign to bring in young voters for the crusade I'm leading. I'm all that stands between the South and the black days of Reconstruction. And you and Tom Junior are going to stand there beside me in the grand crystal ballroom, as shining examples of white Southern youth – in danger.

Heavenly (*defiant*)   Papa, I'm not going to do it.

Boss   I didn't say would you, I said you would, and you will.

Heavenly   Suppose I still say I won't.

Boss   Then you won't, that's all. If you won't, you won't. But there would be consequences you might not like. (*Phone rings.*) Chance Wayne is back in St Cloud.

Charles (*offstage*)   Mr Finley's residence. Miss Heavenly? Sorry, she's not in.

Boss   I'm going to remove him, he's going to be removed from St Cloud. How do you want him to leave, in that white Cadillac he's riding around in, or in the scow that totes the garbage out to the dumping place in the Gulf?

Heavenly   You wouldn't dare!

Boss   You want to take a chance on it?

Charles (*enters*)   That call was for you again, Miss Heavenly.

Boss   A lot of people approve of taking violent action against corrupters. And on all of them that want to adulterate the pure white blood of the South. Hell, when I was fifteen, I come down barefoot out of the red clay hills as if the Voice of God called me. Which it did, I believe. I firmly believe He called me. And nothing, nobody, nowhere is gonna stop me, never . . . (*He motions to* **Charles** *for gift.* **Charles** *hands it to him.*) Thank you, Charles. I'm gonna pay me an early call on Miss Lucy.

A sad, uncertain note has come into his voice on this final line. He turns and plods wearily, doggedly off at left.

The curtain falls.

House remains dark for short intermission.

Scene Two

A corner of cocktail lounge and of outside gallery of the Royal Palms Hotel. This corresponds in style to the bedroom set: Victorian with Moorish influence. Royal palms are projected on the cyclorama which is deep violet with dusk. There are Moorish arches between gallery and interior; over the single table, inside, is suspended the same lamp, stained glass and ornately wrought metal, that hung in the bedroom. Perhaps on the gallery there is a low stone balustrade that supports, where steps descend into the garden, an electric light standard with five branches and pear-shaped globes of a dim pearly luster. Somewhere out of the sightlines an entertainer plays a piano or novachord.

The interior table is occupied by two couples that represent society in St Cloud. They are contemporaries of **Chance**'s. *Behind the bar is* **Stuff** *who feels the dignity of his recent advancement from drugstore soda fountain to the Royal Palms cocktail lounge: he has on a white mess jacket, a scarlet cummerbund and light blue trousers, flatteringly close-fitted.* **Chance Wayne** *was once barman here.* **Stuff** *moves with an indolent male grace that he may have unconsciously remembered admiring in* **Chance**.

Boss Finley's *mistress,* **Miss Lucy**, *enters the cocktail lounge dressed in a ball gown elaborately ruffled and very bouffant like an antebellum Southern belle's. A single blonde curl is arranged to switch girlishly at one side of her sharp little terrier face. She is outraged over something and her glare is concentrated on* **Stuff** *who 'plays it cool' behind the bar.*

Stuff   Ev'nin', Miss Lucy.

Miss Lucy   I wasn't allowed to sit at the banquet table. No. I was put at a little side table, with a couple of state legislators an' wives. (*She sweeps behind the bar in a proprietary fashion.*) Where's your Grant's twelve-year-old? Hey! Do you have a big mouth? I used to remember a kid that jerked sodas at Walgreen's that had a big mouth . . . Put some ice in this . . . Is yours big, huh? I want to tell you something.

Stuff   What's the matter with your finger?

She catches him by his scarlet cummerbund.

Miss Lucy   I'm going to tell you just now. The boss came over to me with a big candy Easter egg for me. The top of the egg unscrewed. He told me to unscrew it. So I unscrewed it. Inside was a little blue velvet jewel box, no not little, a big one, as big as somebody's mouth, too.

Stuff   Whose mouth?

Miss Lucy   The mouth of somebody who's not a hundred miles from here.

Stuff (*going off at the left*)   I got to set my chairs. (**Stuff** *re-enters at once carrying two chairs. Sets them at tables while* **Miss Lucy** *talks.*)

Miss Lucy   I open the jewel box an' start to remove the great big diamond clip in it. I just got my fingers on it, and start to remove it and the old son of a bitch slams the lid of the box on my fingers. One fingernail is still blue. And the boss says to me, 'Now go downstairs to the cocktail lounge and go in the ladies' room and describe this diamond clip with lipstick on the ladies' room mirror down there. Hanh?' – and he put the jewel box in his pocket and slammed the door so hard goin' out of my suite that a picture fell off the wall.

Stuff (*setting the chairs at the table*)   Miss Lucy, you are the one that said, 'I wish you would see what's written with lipstick on the ladies' room mirror' las' Saturday night.

Miss Lucy   To you! Because I thought I could trust you.

Stuff   Other people were here an' all of them heard it.

Miss Lucy   Nobody but you at the bar belonged to the Youth for Boss Finley club.

Both stop short. They've noticed a tall man who has entered the cocktail lounge. He has the length and leanness and luminous pallor of a face that El Greco gave to his saints. He has a small bandage near the hairline. His clothes are country.

Hey, you.

Heckler   Evenin', ma'am.

Miss Lucy   You with the Hillbilly Ramblers? You with the band?

Heckler   I'm a hillbilly, but I'm not with no band.

He notices **Miss Lucy**'s *steady, interested stare.* **Stuff** *leaves with a tray of drinks.*

Miss Lucy   What do you want here?

Heckler   I come to hear Boss Finley talk. (*His voice is clear but strained. He rubs his large Adam's apple as he speaks.*)

Miss Lucy   You can't get in the ballroom without a jacket and a tie on . . . I know who you are. You're the heckler, aren't you?

Heckler   I don't heckle. I just ask questions, one question or two or three questions, depending on how much time it takes them to grab me and throw me out of the hall.

Miss Lucy   Those questions are loaded questions. You gonna repeat them tonight?

Heckler   Yes, ma'am, if I can get in the ballroom, and make myself heard.

Miss Lucy   What's wrong with your voice?

Heckler   When I shouted my questions in New Bethesda last week I got hit in the Adam's apple with the butt of a pistol, and that affected my voice. It still ain't good, but it's better. (*Starts to go.*)

Miss Lucy (*goes to back of bar, where she gets jacket, the kind kept in places with dress regulations, and throws it to* **Heckler**)   Wait. Here, put this on. The Boss's talking on a national TV hookup tonight. There's a tie in the pocket. You sit perfectly still at the bar till the Boss starts speaking. Keep your face back of this *Evening Banner.* OK?

Heckler (*opening the paper in front of his face*)   I thank you.

Miss Lucy   I thank you, too, and I wish you more luck than you're likely to have.

Stuff *re-enters and goes to back of the bar.*

Fly (*entering on the gallery*)   Paging Chance Wayne. (*Auto horn offstage.*) Mr Chance Wayne, please. Paging Chance Wayne. (*He leaves.*)

Miss Lucy (*to* **Stuff** *who has re-entered*)   Is Chance Wayne back in St Cloud?

Stuff   You remember Alexandra Del Lago?

Miss Lucy I guess I do. I was president of her local fan club. Why?

Chance (*offstage*) Hey, boy, park that car up front and don't wrinkle them fenders.

Stuff She and Chance Wayne checked in here last night.

Miss Lucy Well I'll be a dawg's mother. I'm going to look into that. (**Miss Lucy** *exits.*)

Chance (*entering and crossing to the bar*) Hey, Stuff! (*He takes a cocktail off the bar and sips it.*)

Stuff Put that down. This ain't no cocktail party.

Chance Man, don't you know . . . phew . . . nobody drinks gin martinis with olives. Everybody drinks vodka martinis with lemon twist nowadays, except the squares in St Cloud. When I had your job, when I was the barman here at the Royal Palms, I created that uniform you've got on . . . I copied it from an outfit Vic Mature wore in a Foreign Legion picture, and I looked better in it than he did, and almost as good in it as you do, ha, ha . . .

Aunt Nonnie (*who has entered at the right*) Chance. Chance . . .

Chance Aunt Nonnie! (*To* **Stuff**.) Hey, I want a tablecloth on that table, and a bucket of champagne . . . Mumm's Cordon Rouge . . .

Aunt Nonnie You come out here.

Chance But I just ordered champagne in here. (*Suddenly his effusive manner collapses, as she stares at him gravely.*)

Aunt Nonnie I can't be seen talking to you . . .

She leads him to one side of the stage. A light change has occurred which has made it a royal palm grove with a bench. They cross to it solemnly. **Stuff** *busies himself at the bar, which is barely lit. After a moment he exits with a few drinks to main body of the cocktail lounge off left. Bar music. 'Quiereme Mucho'.*

Chance (*following her*) Why?

Aunt Nonnie   I've got just one thing to tell you, Chance, get out of St Cloud.

Chance   Why does everybody treat me like a low criminal in the town I was born in?

Aunt Nonnie   Ask yourself that question, ask your conscience that question.

Chance   What question?

Aunt Nonnie   You know, and I know you know . . .

Chance   Know what?

Aunt Nonnie   I'm not going to talk about it. I just can't talk about it. Your head and your tongue run wild. You can't be trusted. We have to live in St Cloud . . . Oh, Chance, why have you changed like you've changed? Why do you live on nothing but wild dreams now, and have no address where anybody can reach you in time to – reach you?

Chance   Wild dreams! Yes. Isn't life a wild dream? I never heard a better description of it . . . (*He takes a pill and a swallow from a flask.*)

Aunt Nonnie   What did you just take, Chance? You took something out of your pocket and washed it down with liquor.

Chance   Yes, I took a wild dream and – washed it down with another wild dream, Aunt Nonnie, that's my life now . . .

Aunt Nonnie   Why, son?

Chance   Oh, Aunt Nonnie, for God's sake, have you forgotten what was expected of me?

Aunt Nonnie   People that loved you expected just one thing of you – sweetness and honesty and . . .

Stuff *leaves with tray.*

Chance (*kneeling at her side*)   No, not after the brilliant beginning I made. Why, at seventeen, I put on, directed, and played the leading role in *The Valiant,* that one-act play that won the state drama contest. Heavenly played in it with me, and have you forgotten? You went with us as the girls' chaperone to the national contest held in . . .

Aunt Nonnie   Son, of course I remember.

Chance   In the parlor car? How we sang together?

Aunt Nonnie   You were in love even then.

Chance   God, yes, we were in love! (*He sings softly.*)
 'If you like-a me, like I like-a you,
 And we like-a both the same'

Together
 'I'd like-a say, this very day,
 I'd like-a change your name.'

Chance *laughs softly, wildly, in the cool light of the palm grove.* **Aunt Nonnie** *rises abruptly.* **Chance** *catches her hands.*

Aunt Nonnie   You – *do* – take unfair advantage . . .

Chance   Aunt Nonnie, we didn't win that lousy national contest, we just placed second.

Aunt Nonnie   Chance, you didn't place second. You got honorable mention. Fourth place, except it was just called honorable mention.

Chance   Just honorable mention. But in a national contest, honorable mention means something . . . We would have won it, but I blew my lines. Yes, I that put on and produced the damn thing, couldn't even hear the damn lines being hissed at me by that fat girl with the book in the wings. (*He buries his face in his hands.*)

Aunt Nonnie   I loved you for that, son, and so did Heavenly, too.

Chance   It was on the way home in the train that she and I . . .

Aunt Nonnie (*with a flurry of feeling*)   I know, I – I –

Chance (*rising*)   I bribed the Pullman conductor to let us use for an hour a vacant compartment on that sad, home-going train –

Aunt Nonnie   I know, I – I –

Chance   Gave him five dollars, but that wasn't enough, and so I gave him my wrist watch, and my collar pin and tie clip and signet ring and my suit, that I'd bought on credit to go to the contest. First suit I'd ever put on that cost more than thirty dollars.

Aunt Nonnie   Don't go back over that.

Chance   – To buy the first hour of love that we had together. When she undressed, I saw that her body was just then, barely, beginning to be a woman's and . . .

Aunt Nonnie   Stop, Chance.

Chance   I said, oh, Heavenly, no, but she said yes, and I cried in her arms that night, and didn't know that what I was crying for was – youth, that would go.

Aunt Nonnie   It was from that time on, you've changed.

Chance   I swore in my heart that I'd never again come in second in any contest, especially not now that Heavenly was my – Aunt Nonnie, look at this contract. (*He snatches out papers and lights lighter.*)

Aunt Nonnie   I don't want to see false papers.

Chance   These are genuine papers. Look at the notary's seal and the signatures of the three witnesses on them. Aunt Nonnie, do you know who I'm with? I'm with Alexandra Del Lago, the Princess Kosmonopolis is my –

Aunt Nonnie   Is your what?

Chance   Patroness! Agent! Producer! She hasn't been seen much lately, but still has influence, power, and money – money that can open all doors. That I've knocked at all these years till my knuckles are bloody.

Aunt Nonnie   Chance, even now, if you came back here simply saying, 'I couldn't remember the lines, I lost the contest, I – failed,' but you've come back here again with –

Chance   Will you just listen one minute more? Aunt Nonnie, here is the plan. A local-contest-of-Beauty.

Aunt Nonnie   Oh, Chance.

Chance   A local contest of talent that she will win.

Aunt Nonnie   Who?

Chance   Heavenly.

Aunt Nonnie   No, Chance. She's not young now, she's faded, she's . . .

Chance   Nothing goes that quick, not even youth.

Aunt Nonnie   Yes, it does.

Chance   It will come back like magic. Soon as I . . .

Aunt Nonnie   For what? For a fake contest?

Chance   For love. The moment I hold her.

Aunt Nonnie   Chance.

Chance   It's not going to be a local thing, Aunt Nonnie. It's going to get national coverage. The Princess Kosmonopolis's best friend is that sob sister, Sally Powers. Even you know Sally Powers. Most powerful movie columnist in the world. Whose name is law in the motion . . .

Aunt Nonnie   Chance, lower your voice.

Chance   I want people to hear me.

Aunt Nonnie   No, you don't, no you don't. Because if your voice gets to Boss Finley, you'll be in great danger, Chance.

Chance   I go back to Heavenly, or I don't. I live or die. There's nothing in between for me.

Aunt Nonnie   What you want to go back to is your clean, unashamed youth. And you can't.

Chance   You still don't believe me, Aunt Nonnie?

Aunt Nonnie   No, I don't. Please go. Go away from here, Chance.

Chance   Please.

Aunt Nonnie   No, no, go away!

Chance   Where to? Where can I go? This is the home of my heart. Don't make me homeless.

Aunt Nonnie   Oh, Chance.

Chance   Aunt Nonnie. Please.

Aunt Nonnie (*rises and starts to go*)   I'll write to you. Send me an address. I'll write to you.

She exits through bar. **Stuff** *enters and moves to bar.*

Chance   Aunt Nonnie . . .

She's gone.

Chance *removes a pint bottle of vodka from his pocket and something else which he washes down with the vodka. He stands back as two couples come up the steps and cross the gallery into the bar; they sit at a table.* **Chance** *takes a deep breath.* **Fly** *enters lighted area inside, singing out 'Paging Mr Chance Wayne, Mr Chance Wayne, pagin' Mr Chance Wayne.' Turns about smartly and goes back out through lobby. The name has stirred a commotion at the bar and table visible inside.*

Edna   Did you hear *that*? Is *Chance Wayne* back in St Cloud? (**Chance** *draws a deep breath. Then, he stalks back into the main part of the cocktail lounge like a matador entering a bull ring.*)

Violet   My God, yes – there he is.

Chance *reads* **Fly***'s message.*

Chance (*to* **Fly**)   Not now, later, later.

The entertainer off left begins to play a piano . . . The 'evening' in the cocktail lounge is just beginning.

Fly *leaves through the gallery.*

Chance   Well! Same old place, same old gang. Time doesn't pass in St Cloud. (*To* **Bud** *and* **Scotty**.) Hi!

Bud   How are you . . .

Chance (*shouting offstage*)   Hey, Jackie . . . (**Fly** *enters and stands on terrace. Piano stops.* **Chance** *crosses over to the table that holds the foursome.*) . . . remember my song? Do you – remember my song? . . . You see, he remembers my song. (*The entertainer swings into 'It's a Big Wide Wonderful World'.*) Now I feel at home. In my home town . . . Come on, everybody – sing!

This token of apparent acceptance reassures him. The foursome at the table on stage studiously ignore him. He sings:

Chance
  'When you're in love you're a master
  Of all you survey, you're a gay Santa Claus.
  There's a great big star-spangled sky up above you,
  When you're in love you're a hero . . . '

Come on! Sing, ev'rybody!

~~In the old days they did; now they don't.~~ *He goes on, singing a bit; then his voice dies out on a note of embarrassment. Somebody at the bar whispers something and another laughs.* **Chance** *chuckles uneasily and says:*

What's wrong here? The place is dead.

Stuff   You been away too long, Chance.

Chance   Is that the trouble?

Stuff   That's all . . .

Jackie, *off, finishes with an arpeggio. The piano slams. There is a curious hush in the bar.* **Chance** *looks at the table.* **Violet** *whispers something to* **Bud**. *Both girls rise abruptly and cross out of the bar.*

Bud (*yelling at* **Stuff**)   Check, Stuff.

Chance (*with exaggerated surprise*)   Well, *Bud and Scotty.* I didn't see you at all. Wasn't that Violet and Edna at your table? (*He sits at the table between* **Bud** *and* **Scotty**.)

Scotty   I guess they didn't recognize you, Chance.

Bud   Violet did.

Scotty   Did Violet?

Bud   She said, 'My God, Chance Wayne.'

Scotty   That's recognition and profanity, too.

Chance   I don't mind. I've been snubbed by experts, and I've done some snubbing myself . . . Hey! (**Miss Lucy** *has entered at left.* **Chance** *sees her and goes toward her.*) Is that Miss Lucy or is that Scarlett O'Hara?

Miss Lucy   Hello there, Chance Wayne. Somebody said that you were back in St Cloud, but I didn't believe them. I said I'd have to see it with my own eyes before . . . Usually there's an item in the paper, in Gwen Phillips's column saying 'St Cloud youth home on visit is slated to play featured role in important new picture', and me being a movie fan I'm always thrilled by it . . . (*She ruffles his hair.*)

Chance   Never do that to a man with thinning hair. (**Chance**'s *smile is unflinching; it gets harder and brighter.*)

Miss Lucy   Is your hair thinning, baby? Maybe that's the difference I noticed in your appearance. Don't go 'way till I get back with my drink . . .

She goes to back of bar to mix herself a drink. Meanwhile, **Chance** *combs his hair.*

Scotty (*to* **Chance**)   Don't throw away those golden hairs you combed out, Chance. Save 'em and send 'em each in letters to your fan clubs.

Bud   Does Chance Wayne have a fan club?

Scotty   The most patient one in the world. They've been waiting years for him to show up on the screen for more than five seconds in a crowd scene.

Miss Lucy (*returning to the table*)   Y'know this boy Chance Wayne used to be so attractive I couldn't stand it. But now I can, almost stand it. Every Sunday in summer I used to drive out to the municipal beach and watch him dive off the high tower. I'd take binoculars with me when he put on those free divin' exhibitions. You still dive, Chance? Or have you given that up?

Chance (*uneasily*)   I did some diving last Sunday.

Miss Lucy   Good, as ever?

Chance   I was a little off form, but the crowd didn't notice. I can still get away with a double back somersault and a –

Miss Lucy   Where was this, in Palm Beach, Florida, Chance? (**Hatcher** *enters.*)

Chance (*stiffening*)   Why Palm Beach? Why there?

Miss Lucy   Who was it said they seen you last month in Palm Beach? Oh yes, Hatcher – that you had a job as a beach-boy at some big hotel there?

Hatcher (*stops at steps of the terrace, then leaves across the gallery*) Yeah, that's what I heard.

Chance   Had a job – as a beach-boy?

Stuff   Rubbing oil into big fat millionaires.

Chance   What joker thought up that one? (*His laugh is a little too loud.*)

Scotty   You ought to get their names and sue them for slander.

Chance   I long ago gave up tracking down sources of rumors about me. Of course, it's flattering, it's gratifying to know that you're still being talked about in your old home town, even if what they say is completely fantastic. Hahaha.

Entertainer returns, sweeps into 'Quiereme Mucho'.

Miss Lucy   Baby, you've changed in some way, but I can't put my finger on it. You all see a change in him, or has he just gotten older? (*She sits down next to* **Chance**.)

Chance (*quickly*) To change is to live, Miss Lucy, to live is to change, and not to change is to die. You know that, don't you? It used to scare me sometimes. I'm not scared of it now. Are you scared of it, Miss Lucy? Does it scare you?

Behind **Chance**'s *back one of the girls has appeared and signaled the boys to join them outside.* **Scotty** *nods and holds up two fingers to mean they'll come in a couple of minutes. The girl goes back out with an angry head-toss.*

Scotty Chance, did you know Boss Finley was holding a Youth for Tom Finley rally upstairs tonight?

Chance I saw the announcements of it all over town.

Bud He's going to state his position on that emasculation business that's stirred up such a mess in the state. Had you heard about that?

Chance No.

Scotty He must have been up in some earth satellite if he hasn't heard about that.

Chance No, just out of St Cloud.

Scotty Well, they picked out a nigger at random and castrated the bastard to show they mean business about white women's protection in this state.

Bud Some people think they went too far about it. There's been a whole lot of Northern agitation all over the country.

Scotty The Boss is going to state his own position about that thing before the Youth for Boss Finley rally upstairs in the Crystal Ballroom.

Chance Aw. Tonight?

Stuff Yeah, t'night.

Bud They say that Heavenly Finley and Tom Junior are going to be standing on the platform with him.

Pageboy (*entering*) Paging Chance Wayne. Paging . . . (*He is stopped short by* **Edna**.)

Chance   I *doubt* that story, somehow I *doubt* that story.

Stuff   You doubt they cut that nigger?

Chance   Oh, no, that I don't doubt. You know what that is, don't you? Sex-envy is what that is, and the revenge for sex-envy which is a widespread disease that I have run into personally too often for me to doubt its existence or any manifestation. (*The group push back their chairs, snubbing him.* **Chance** *takes the message from the* **Pageboy**, *reads it and throws it on the floor.*) Hey, Stuff! – What d'ya have to do, stand on your head to get a drink around here? – Later, tell her. – Miss Lucy, can you get that Walgreen's soda jerk to give me a shot of vodka on the rocks? (*She snaps her fingers at* **Stuff**. *He shrugs and sloshes some vodka onto ice.*)

Miss Lucy   Chance? You're too loud, baby.

Chance   Not loud enough, Miss Lucy. No. What I meant that I doubt is that Heavenly Finley, that only I know in St Cloud, would stoop to stand on a platform next to her father while he explains and excuses on TV this random emasculation of a young Nigra caught on a street after midnight. (**Chance** *is speaking with an almost incoherent excitement, one knee resting on the seat of his chair, swaying the chair back and forth. The* **Heckler** *lowers his newspaper from his face; a slow fierce smile spreads over his face as he leans forward with tensed throat muscles to catch* **Chance***'s burst of oratory.*) No! That's what I do not believe. If I believed it, oh, I'd give you a diving exhibition. I'd dive off municipal pier and swim straight out to Diamond Key and past it, and keep on swimming till sharks and barracuda took me for live bait, brother. (*His chair topples over backward, and he sprawls to the floor. The* **Heckler** *springs up to catch him.* **Miss Lucy** *springs up too, and sweeps between* **Chance** *and the* **Heckler**, *pushing the* **Heckler** *back with a quick, warning look or gesture. Nobody notices the* **Heckler**. **Chance** *scrambles back to his feet, flushed, laughing.* **Bud** *and* **Scotty** *outlaugh him.* **Chance** *picks up his chair and continues. The laughter stops.*) Because I have come back to St Cloud to take her out of St Cloud. Where I'll take her is not to a place anywhere except to her place in my heart. (*He has removed a pink* *capsule from his pocket, quickly and furtively, and drunk it down with his vodka.)*

Bud   Chance, what did you swallow just now?

Chance   Some hundred-proof vodka.

Bud   You washed something down with it that you took out of your pocket.

Scotty   It looked like a little pink pill.

Chance   Oh, ha ha. Yes, I washed down a goof-ball. You want one? I got a bunch of them. I always carry them with me. When you're not having fun, it makes you have it. When you're having fun, it makes you have more of it. Have one and see.

Scotty   Don't that damage the brain?

Chance   No, the contrary. It stimulates the brain cells.

Scotty   Don't it make your eyes look different, Chance?

Miss Lucy   Maybe that's what I noticed. (*As if wishing to change the subject.*) Chance, I wish you'd settle an argument for me.

Chance   What argument, Miss Lucy?

Miss Lucy   About who you're traveling with. I heard you checked in here with a famous old movie star.

They all stare at him . . . In a way he now has what he wants. He's the center of attraction: everybody is looking at him, even though with hostility, suspicion and a cruel sense of sport.

Chance   Miss Lucy, I'm traveling with the vice-president and major stockholder of the film studio which just signed me.

Miss Lucy   Wasn't she once in the movies and very well known?

Chance   She was and still is and never will cease to be an important, a legendary figure in the picture industry, here and all over the world, and I am now under personal contract to her.

Miss Lucy   What's her name, Chance?

Chance   She doesn't want her name known. Like all great figures, world-known, she doesn't want or need and refuses to have the wrong type of attention. Privacy is a luxury to great stars. Don't ask me her name. I respect her too much to speak her name at this table. I'm obligated to her because she has shown faith in me. It took a long hard time to find that sort of faith in my talent that this woman has shown me. And I refuse to betray it at this table. (*His voice rises; he is already 'high'.*)

Miss Lucy   Baby, why are you sweating and your hands shaking so? You're not sick, are you?

Chance   Sick? Who's sick? I'm the least sick one you know.

Miss Lucy   Well, baby, you know you oughtn't to stay in St Cloud. Y'know that, don't you? I couldn't believe my ears when I heard you were back here. (*To the two boys.*) Could you all believe he was back here?

Scotty   What did you come back for?

Chance   I wish you would give me one reason why I shouldn't come back to visit the grave of my mother and pick out a monument for her, and share my happiness with a girl that I've loved many years. It's her, Heavenly Finley, that I've fought my way up for, and now that I've made it, the glory will be hers, too. And I've just about persuaded the powers to be to let her appear with me in a picture I'm signed for. Because I . . .

Bud   What is the name of this picture?

Chance   . . . Name of it? *Youth*!

Bud   Just *Youth*?

Chance   Isn't that a great title for a picture introducing young talent? You all look doubtful. If you don't believe me, well, look. Look at this contract. (*Removes it from his pocket.*)

Scotty   You carry the contract with you?

Chance   I happen to have it in this jacket pocket.

Miss Lucy   Leaving, Scotty? (**Scotty** *has risen from the table.*)

Scotty   It's getting too deep at this table.

Bud   The girls are waiting.

Chance (*quickly*)   Gee, Bud, that's a clean set of rags you're wearing, but let me give you a tip for your tailor. A guy of medium stature looks better with natural shoulders, the padding cuts down your height, it broadens your figure and gives you a sort of squat look.

Bud   Thanks, Chance.

Scotty   You got any helpful hints for my tailor, Chance?

Chance   Scotty, there's no tailor on earth that can disguise a sedentary occupation.

Miss Lucy   Chance, baby . . .

Chance   You still work down at the bank? You sit on your can all day countin' century notes and once every week they let you slip one in your pockets? That's a fine setup, Scotty, if you're satisfied with it but it's starting to give you a little pot and a can.

Violet (*appears in the door, angry*)   Bud! Scotty! Come on.

Scotty   I don't get by on my looks, but I drive my own car. It isn't a Caddy, but it's my own car. And if my own mother died, I'd bury her myself; I wouldn't let a church take up a collection to do it.

Violet (*impatiently*)   Scotty, if you all don't come now I'm going home in a taxi.

The two boys follow her into the Palm Garden. There they can be seen giving their wives cab money, and indicating they are staying.

Chance   The squares have left us, Miss Lucy.

Miss Lucy   Yeah.

Chance   Well . . . I didn't come back here to fight with old friends of mine . . . Well, it's quarter past seven.

Miss Lucy   Is it?

*There are a number of men, now, sitting around in the darker corners of
the bar, looking at him. They are not ominous in their attitudes. They are
simply waiting for something, for the meeting to start upstairs, for
something . . .* **Miss Lucy** *stares at* **Chance** *and the men, then again
at* **Chance**, *nearsightedly, her head cocked like a puzzled terrier's.*
Chance *is discomfited.*

Chance   Yep . . . How is that Hickory Hollow for steaks? Is
it still the best place in town for a steak?

Stuff (*answering the phone at the bar*)   Yeah, it's him. He's here.
(*Looks at* **Chance** *ever so briefly, hangs up.*)

Miss Lucy   Baby, I'll go to the checkroom and pick up my
wrap and call for my car and I'll drive you out to the airport.
They've got an air-taxi out there, a whirly-bird taxi, a
helicopter, you know, that'll hop you to New Orleans in fifteen
minutes.

Chance   I'm not leaving St Cloud. What did I say to make
you think I was?

Miss Lucy   I thought you had sense enough to know that
you'd better.

Chance   Miss Lucy, you've been drinking, it's gone to your
sweet little head.

Miss Lucy   Think it over while I'm getting my wrap. You
still got a friend in St Cloud.

Chance   I still have a girl in St Cloud, and I'm not leaving
without her.

Pageboy (*offstage*)   Paging Chance Wayne, Mr Chance Wayne,
please.

Princess (*entering with* **Pageboy**)   Louder, young man,
louder . . . Oh, never mind, here he is!

But **Chance** *has already rushed out onto the gallery. The* **Princess**
*looks as if she had thrown on her clothes to escape a building on fire. Her
blue-sequined gown is unzipped, or partially zipped, her hair is disheveled,
her eyes have a dazed, drugged brightness; she is holding up the eyeglasses*

with the broken lens, shakily, hanging onto her mink stole with the other hand; her movements are unsteady.

Miss Lucy   I know who you are. Alexandra Del Lago. (*Loud whispering. A pause.*)

Princess (*on the step to the gallery*)   What? Chance!

Miss Lucy   Honey, let me fix that zipper for you. Hold still just a second. Honey, let me take you upstairs. You mustn't be seen down here in this condition . . .

Chance *suddenly rushes in from the gallery: he conducts the* **Princess** *outside: she is on the verge of panic. The* **Princess** *rushes half down the steps to the Palm Garden; leans panting on the stone balustrade under the ornamental light standard with its five great pearls of light. The interior is dimmed as* **Chance** *comes out behind her.*

Princess   Chance! Chance! Chance! Chance!

Chance (*softly*)   If you'd stayed upstairs that wouldn't have happened to you.

Princess   I did, I stayed.

Chance   I told you to wait.

Princess   I waited.

Chance   Didn't I tell you to wait till I got back?

Princess   I did, I waited forever, I waited forever for you. Then finally I heard those long sad silver trumpets blowing through the Palm Garden and then – Chance, the most wonderful thing has happened to me. Will you listen to me? Will you let me tell you?

Miss Lucy (*to the group at the bar*)   Shhh!

Princess   Chance, when I saw you driving under the window with your head held high, with that terrible stiff-necked pride of the defeated which I know so well; I knew that your comeback had been a failure like mine. And I felt something in my heart for you. That's a miracle, Chance. That's the wonderful thing that happened to me. I felt something for someone besides myself. That means my heart's still alive, at least some part of it is, not all of my heart is dead yet. Part's alive still . . . Chance, please listen to me. I'm ashamed of this morning. I'll never degrade you again, I'll never degrade myself, you and me, again by – I wasn't always this monster. Once I wasn't this monster. And what I felt in my heart when I saw you returning, defeated, to this palm garden, Chance, gave me hope that I could stop being a monster. Chance, you've got to help me stop being the monster that I was this morning, and you can do it, can help me. I won't be ungrateful for it. I almost died this morning, suffocated in a panic. But even through my panic, I saw your kindness. I saw a true kindness in you that you have almost destroyed, but that's still there, a little . . .

Chance   What kind thing did I do?

Princess   You gave my oxygen to me.

Chance   Anyone would do that.

Princess   It could háve taken you longer to give it to me.

Chance   I'm not that kind of monster.

Princess   You're no kind of monster. You're just –

Chance   What?

Princess   Lost in the beanstalk country, the ogre's country at the top of the beanstalk, the country of the flesh-hungry, blood-thirsty ogre –

Suddenly a voice is heard from off.

Voice   Wayne?

The call is distinct but not loud. **Chance** *hears it, but doesn't turn toward it; he freezes momentarily, like a stag scenting hunters. Among the people gathered inside in the cocktail lounge we see the speaker,* **Dan Hatcher**. *In appearance, dress and manner he is the apotheosis of the assistant hotel manager, about* **Chance**'s *age, thin, blond-haired, trim blond mustache, suave, boyish, betraying an instinct for murder only by the ruby-glass studs in his matching cuff links and tie clip.*

Hatcher   Wayne!

He steps forward a little and at the same instant **Tom Junior** *and* **Scotty** *appear behind him, just in view.* **Scotty** *strikes a match for* **Tom Junior***'s cigarette as they wait there.* **Chance** *suddenly gives the* **Princess** *his complete and tender attention, putting an arm around her and turning her toward the Moorish arch to the bar entrance.*

Chance (*loudly*)   I'll get you a drink, and then I'll take you upstairs. You're not well enough to stay down here.

Hatcher (*crossing quickly to the foot of the stairs*)   Wayne!

The call is too loud to ignore. **Chance** *half turns and calls back.*

Chance   Who's that?

Hatcher   Step down here a minute!

Chance   Oh, *Hatcher*! I'll be right with you.

Princess   Chance, don't leave me alone.

At this moment the arrival of **Boss Finley** *is heralded by the sirens of several squad cars. The forestage is suddenly brightened from off left, presumably the floodlights of the cars arriving at the entrance to the hotel. This is the signal the men at the bar have been waiting for. Everybody rushes off left. In the hot light all alone on stage is* **Chance***; behind him is the* **Princess***. And the* **Heckler** *is at the bar. The entertainer plays a feverish tango. Now, off left,* **Boss Finley** *can be heard, his public personality very much 'on'. Amid the flash of flash bulbs we hear off:*

Boss (*off*)   Hahaha! Little Bit, smile! Go on, smile for the birdie! Ain't she Heavenly, ain't that the right name for her!

Heavenly (*off*)   Papa, I want to go in!

At this instant she runs in – to face **Chance** . . . *The* **Heckler** *rises. For a long instant,* **Chance** *and* **Heavenly** *stand there: he on the steps leading to the Palm Garden and gallery; she in the cocktail lounge. They simply look at each other* . . . *the* **Heckler** *between them. Then the* **Boss** *comes in and seizes her by the arm* . . . *And there he is facing the* **Heckler** *and* **Chance** *both* . . . *For a split second he faces them, half lifts his cane to strike at them, but doesn't strike* . . . *then pulls* **Heavenly** *back off left stage* . . . *where the photographing and interviews* *proceed during what follows.* **Chance** *has seen that* **Heavenly** *is going to go on the platform with her father . . . He stands there stunned . . .*

Princess   Chance! Chance? (*He turns to her blindly.*) Call the car and let's go. Everything's packed, even the . . . tape recorder with my shameless voice on it . . .

The **Heckler** *has returned to his position at the bar. Now* **Hatcher** *and* **Scotty** *and a couple of other of the boys have come out . . . The* **Princess** *sees them and is silent . . . She's never been in anything like this before . . .*

Hatcher   Wayne, step down here, will you.

Chance   What for, what do you want?

Hatcher   Come down here, I'll tell you.

Chance   You come up here and tell me.

Tom Junior   Come on, you chicken-gut bastard.

Chance   Why, hello, Tom Junior. Why are you hiding down there?

Tom Junior   You're hiding, not me, chicken-gut.

Chance   You're in the dark, not me.

Hatcher   Tom Junior wants to talk to you privately down here.

Chance   He can talk to me privately up here.

Tom Junior   Hatcher, tell him I'll talk to him in the washroom on the mezzanine floor.

Chance   I don't hold conversations with people in washrooms . . .

Tom Junior *infuriated, starts to rush forward. Men restrain him.*

Chance   What is all this anyhow? It's fantastic. You all having a little conference there? I used to leave places when I was told to. Not now. That time's over. Now I leave when I'm ready. Hear that, Tom Junior? Give your father that message. This is my town. I was born in St Cloud, not him. He was just called here. He was just called down from the hills to preach hate. I was born here to make love. Tell him about that difference between him and me, and ask him which he thinks has more right to stay here . . . (*He gets no answer from the huddled little group which is restraining* **Tom Junior** *from perpetrating murder right there in the cocktail lounge. After all, that would be a bad incident to precede the* **Boss**'s *all-South-wide TV appearance . . . and they all know it.* **Chance**, *at the same time, continues to taunt them.*) Tom, Tom Junior! What do you want me for? To pay me back for the ball game and picture show money I gave you when you were cutting your father's yard grass for a dollar on Saturday? Thank me for the times I gave you my motorcycle and got you a girl to ride the buddy seat with you? Come here! I'll give you the keys to my Caddy. I'll give you the price of any whore in St Cloud. You still got credit with me because you're Heavenly's brother.

Tom Junior (*almost bursting free*) Don't say the name of my sister!

Chance I said the name of my girl!

Tom Junior (*breaking away from the group*) I'm all right, I'm all right. Leave us alone, will you. I don't want Chance to feel that he's outnumbered. (*He herds them out.*) OK? Come on down here.

Princess (*trying to restrain* **Chance**) No, Chance, don't.

Tom Junior Excuse yourself from the lady and come on down here. Don't be scared to. I just want to talk to you quietly. Just talk. Quiet talk.

Chance Tom Junior, I know that since the last time I was here something has happened to Heavenly and I –

Tom Junior Don't – speak the name of my sister. Just leave her name off your tongue –

Chance Just tell me what happened to her.

Tom Junior Keep your ruttin' voice down.

Chance I know I've done many wrong things in my life, many more than I can name or number, but I swear I never hurt Heavenly in my life.

Tom Junior   You mean to say my sister was had by somebody else – diseased by somebody else the last time you were in St Cloud? . . . I know, it's possible, it's barely possible that you didn't know what you done to my little sister the last time you come to St Cloud. You remember that time when you came home broke? My sister had to pick up your tabs in restaurants and bars, and had to cover bad checks you wrote on banks where you had no accounts. Until you met this rich bitch, Minnie, the Texas one with the yacht, and started spending weekends on her yacht, and coming back Mondays with money from Minnie to go on with my sister. I mean, you'd sleep with Minnie, that slept with any goddam gigolo bastard she could pick up on Bourbon Street or the docks, and then you would go on sleeping again with my sister. And some time, during that time, you got something besides your gigolo fee from Minnie and passed it on to my sister, my little sister that had hardly even heard of a thing like that, and didn't know what it was till it had gone on too long and –

Chance   I left town before I found out I –

'The Lamentation' is heard.

Tom Junior   You found out! Did you tell my little sister?

Chance   I thought if something was wrong she'd write me or call me –

Tom Junior   How could she write you or call you, there're no addresses, no phone numbers in gutters. I'm itching to kill you – here, on this spot! . . . My little sister, Heavenly, didn't know about the diseases and operations of whores, till she had to be cleaned and cured – I mean spayed like a dawg by Dr George Scudder's knife. That's right – by the knife! . . . And tonight – if you stay here tonight, if you're here after this rally, you're gonna get the knife, too. You know? The knife? That's all. Now go on back to the lady, I'm going back to my father. (**Tom Junior** *exits.*)

Princess (*as* **Chance** *returns to her*)   Chance, for God's sake, let's go now . . .

'The Lament' is in the air. It blends with the wind-blown sound of the palms.

All day I've kept hearing a sort of lament that drifts through the air of this place. It says, 'Lost, lost, never to be found again.' Palm gardens by the sea and olive groves on Mediterranean islands all have that lament drifting through them. 'Lost, lost' . . . The isle of Cyprus, Monte Carlo, San Remo, Torremolinos, Tangiers. They're all places of exile from whatever we loved. Dark glasses, wide-brimmed hats and whispers, 'Is that her?' Shocked whispers . . . Oh, Chance, believe me, after failure comes flight. Nothing ever comes after failure but flight. Face it. Call the car, have them bring down the luggage and let's go on along the Old Spanish Trail. (*She tries to hold him.*)

Chance   Keep your grabbing hands off me. (*Marchers offstage start to sing 'Bonnie Blue Flag'.*)

Princess   There's no one but me to hold you back from destruction in this place.

Chance   I don't want to be held.

Princess   Don't leave me. If you do I'll turn into the monster again. I'll be the first lady of the Beanstalk Country.

Chance   Go back to the room.

Princess   I'm going nowhere alone. I can't.

Chance (*in desperation*)   Wheel chair! (*Marchers enter from the left,* **Tom Junior** *and* **Boss** *with them.*) Wheel chair! Stuff, get the lady a wheel chair! She's having another attack!

Stuff *and a* **Bellboy** *catch at her . . . but she pushes* **Chance** *away and stares at him reproachfully . . . The* **Bellboy** *takes her by the arm. She accepts this anonymous arm and exits.* **Chance** *and the* **Heckler** *are alone on stage.*

Chance (*as if reassuring, comforting somebody besides himself*)   It's all right, I'm alone now, nobody's hanging onto me.

He is panting. Loosens his tie and collar. Band in the Crystal Ballroom, muted, strikes up a lively but lyrically distorted variation of some such popular tune as the 'Liechtensteiner Polka'. **Chance** *turns toward the sound. Then, from left stage, comes a drum majorette, bearing a gold and purple silk banner inscribed 'Youth for Tom Finley', prancing and followed by* **Boss Finley**, **Heavenly** *and* **Tom Junior**, *with a tight grip on her arm, as if he were conducting her to a death chamber.*

Tom Junior   Papa? Papa! Will you tell Sister to march?

Boss Finley   Little Bit, you hold your haid up *high* when we march into that ballroom. (*Music up high . . . They march up the steps and onto the gallery in the rear . . . then start across it. The* **Boss** *calling out:*) Now march! (*And they disappear up the stairs.*)

Voice (*offstage*)   Now let us pray. (*There is a prayer mumbled by many voices.*)

Miss Lucy (*who has remained behind*)   You still want to try it?

Heckler   I'm going to take a shot at it. How's my voice?

Miss Lucy   Better.

Heckler   I better wait here till he starts talkin', huh?

Miss Lucy   Wait till they turn down the chandeliers in the ballroom . . . Why don't you switch to a question that won't hurt his daughter?

Heckler   I don't want to hurt his daughter. But he's going to hold her up as the fair white virgin exposed to black lust in the South, and that's his build-up, his lead into his Voice of God speech.

Miss Lucy   He honestly believes it.

Heckler   I don't believe it. I believe that the silence of God, the absolute speechlessness of Him, is a long, long and awful thing that the whole world is lost because of. I think it's yet to be broken to any man, living or any yet lived on earth – no exceptions, and least of all Boss Finley.

Stuff *enters, goes to table, starts to wipe it. The chandelier lights go down.*

Miss Lucy (*with admiration*)   It takes a hillbilly to cut down a hillbilly . . . (*To* **Stuff**.) Turn on the television, baby.

Voice (*offstage*)   I give you the beloved Thomas J. Finley.

Stuff *makes a gesture as if to turn on the TV, which we play in the fourth wall. A wavering beam of light, flickering, narrow, intense, comes from the balcony rail.* **Stuff** *moves his head so that he's in it, looking into it . . .* **Chance** *walks slowly downstage, his head also in the narrow flickering beam of light. As he walks downstage, there suddenly appears on the big TV screen, which is the whole back wall of the stage, the image of* **Boss Finley**. *His arm is around* **Heavenly** *and he is speaking . . . When* **Chance** *sees the* **Boss**'*s arm around* **Heavenly**, *he makes a noise in his throat like a hard fist hit him low . . . Now the sound, which always follows the picture by an instant, comes on . . . loud.*

Boss (*on TV screen*)   Thank you, my friends, neighbors, kinfolk, fellow Americans . . . I have told you before, but I will tell you again. I got a mission that I hold sacred to perform in the Southland. When I was fifteen I came down barefooted out of the red clay hills. Why? Because the Voice of God called me to execute this mission.

Miss Lucy (*to* **Stuff**)   He's too loud.

Heckler   Listen!

Boss   And what is this mission? I have told you before but I will tell you again. To shield from pollution a blood that I think is not only sacred to me, but sacred to Him.

Upstage we see the **Heckler** *step up the last steps and make a gesture as if he were throwing doors open . . . He advances into the hall, out of our sight.*

Miss Lucy   Turn it down, Stuff.

Stuff (*motioning to her*)   Shh!

Boss   Who is the colored man's best friend in the South? That's right . . .

Miss Lucy   Stuff, turn down the volume.

Boss   It's me, Tom Finley. So recognized by both races.

Stuff (*shouting*)   He's speaking the word. Pour it on!

Boss   However – I can't and will not accept, tolerate, condone this threat of a blood pollution.

Miss Lucy *turns down the volume of the TV set.*

TV:

Boss   As you all know I had no part in a certain operation on a young black gentleman. I call that incident a deplorable thing. That is the one thing about which I am in total agreement with the Northern radical press. It was a de-plor-able thing. However . . . I understand the emotions that lay behind it. The passion to protect by this violent emotion something that we hold sacred: our purity of our own blood! But I had no part in, and I did not condone the operation performed on the unfortunate colored gentleman caught prowling the midnight streets of our Capitol City . . .

Live:

Chance   Christ! What lies. What a liar!

Miss Lucy   Wait! . . . Chance, you can still go. I can still help you, baby.

Chance (*putting hands on* **Miss Lucy***'s shoulders*) Thanks, but no thank you, Miss Lucy. Tonight, God help me, somehow, I don't know how, but somehow I'll take her out of St Cloud. I'll wake her up in my arms, and I'll give her life back to her. Yes, somehow, God help me, somehow!

Stuff *turns up volume of TV set.*

Heckler (*as voice on the TV*)   Hey, Boss Finley! (*The TV camera swings to show him at the back of the hall.*) How about your daughter's operation? How about that operation your daughter had done on her at the Thomas J. Finley hospital here in St Cloud? Did she put on black in mourning for her appendix? . . .

We hear a gasp, as if the **Heckler** *had been hit. Picture:* **Heavenly** *horrified. Sounds of a disturbance. Then the doors at the top stairs up left burst open and the* **Heckler** *tumbles down . . . The picture changes to* **Boss Finley***. He is trying to dominate the disturbance in the hall.*

Boss   Will you repeat that question. Have that man step forward. I will answer his question. Where is he? Have that man step forward, I will answer his question . . . Last Friday . . . Last Friday, Good Friday. I said last Friday, Good Friday . . . Quiet, may I have your attention please . . . Last Friday, Good Friday, I seen a horrible thing on the campus of our great State University, which I built for the state. A hideous straw-stuffed effigy of myself, Tom Finley, was hung and set fire to in the main quadrangle of the college. This outrage was inspired . . . inspired by the Northern radical press. However, that was Good Friday. Today is Easter. I say that was Good Friday. Today is Easter Sunday and I am in St Cloud.

During this a gruesome, ~~not lighted~~, silent struggle has been going on. The **Heckler** *defended himself, but finally has been overwhelmed and rather systematically beaten . . . The tight intense follow-spot beam stayed on* **Chance**. *If he had any impulse to go to the* **Heckler**'s *aid, he'd be discouraged by* **Stuff** *and another man who stand behind him, watching him . . . At the height of the beating, there are bursts of great applause . . . At a point during it,* **Heavenly** *is suddenly escorted down the stairs, sobbing, and collapses . . .*

Curtain.

Act Three

A while later that night: the hotel bedroom. The shutters in the Moorish corner are thrown open on the Palm Garden: scattered sounds of disturbance are still heard; something burns in the Palm Garden: an effigy, an emblem? Flickering light from it falls on the **Princess**. *Over the interior scene, the constant serene projection of royal palms, branched among stars.*

Princess (*pacing with the phone*)   Operator! What's happened to my driver?

Chance *enters on the gallery, sees someone approaching on other side – quickly pulls back and stands in shadows on the gallery.*

Princess   You told me you'd get me a driver . . . Why can't you get me a driver when you said that you would? Somebody in this hotel can surely get me somebody to drive me at any price asked! – out of this infernal . . .

She turns suddenly as **Dan Hatcher** *knocks at the corridor door. Behind him appear* **Tom Junior**, **Bud** *and* **Scotty**, *sweaty, disheveled from the riot in the Palm Garden.*

Princess   Who's that?

Scotty   She ain't gonna open, break it in.

Princess (*dropping phone*)   What do you want?

Hatcher   Miss Del Lago . . .

Bud   Don't answer till she opens.

Princess   Who's out there! What do you want?

Scotty (*to shaky* **Hatcher**)   Tell her you want her out of the goddam room.

Hatcher (*with forced note of authority*)   Shut up. Let me handle this . . . Miss Del Lago, your check-out time was three-thirty p.m., and it's now after midnight . . . I'm sorry but you can't hold this room any longer.

Princess (*throwing open the door*)   What did you say? Will you repeat what you said! (*Her imperious voice, jewels, furs and commanding presence abash them for a moment.*)

Hatcher   Miss Del Lago . . .

Tom Junior (*recovering quickest*)   This is Mr Hatcher, assistant manager here. You checked in last night with a character not wanted here, and we been informed he's stayin' in your room with you. We brought Mr Hatcher up here to remind you that the check-out time is long past and –

Princess (*powerfully*)   My check-out time at any hotel in the world is *when I want to check out* . . .

Tom Junior   This ain't any hotel in the world.

Princess (*making no room for entrance*)   Also, I don't talk to assistant managers of hotels when I have complaints to make about discourtesies to me, which I do most certainly have to make about my experiences here. I don't even talk to managers of hotels, I talk to owners of them. Directly to hotel owners about discourtesies to me. (*Picks up satin sheets on bed.*) These sheets are mine, they go with me. And I have never suffered such dreadful discourtesies to me at any hotel at any time or place anywhere in the world. Now I have found out the name of this hotel owner. This is a chain hotel under the ownership of a personal friend of mine whose guest I have been in foreign capitals such as . . . (**Tom Junior** *has pushed past her into the room.*) What in hell is he doing in my room?

Tom Junior   Where is Chance Wayne?

Princess   Is that what you've come here for? You can go away then. He hasn't been in this room since he left this morning.

Tom Junior   Scotty, check the bathroom . . . (*He checks a closet, stoops to peer under the bed.* **Scotty** *goes off at right.*) Like I told you before, we know you're Alexandra Del Lago traveling with a degenerate that I'm sure you don't know. That's why you can't stay in St Cloud, especially after this ruckus that we – (**Scotty** *re-enters from the bathroom and indicates to* **Tom Junior**

that **Chance** *is not there.*) – Now if you need any help in getting out of St Cloud, I'll be –

Princess (*cutting in*)   Yes. I want a driver. Someone to drive my car. I want to leave here. I'm desperate to leave here. I'm not able to drive. I have to be driven away!

Tom Junior   Scotty, you and Hatcher wait outside while I explain something to her . . . (*They go and wait outside the door, on the left end of the gallery.*) I'm gonna git you a driver, Miss Del Lago. I'll git you a state trooper, half a dozen state troopers if I can't get you no driver. OK? Some time come back to our town n' see us, hear? We'll lay out a red carpet for you. OK? G'night, Miss Del Lago.

They disappear down the hall, which is then dimmed out. **Chance** *now turns from where he's been waiting at the other end of the corridor and slowly, cautiously, approaches the entrance to the room. Wind sweeps the Palm Garden; it seems to dissolve the walks; the rest of the play is acted against the night sky. The shuttered doors on the veranda open and* **Chance** *enters the room. He has gone a good deal further across the border of reason since we last saw him. The* **Princess** *isn't aware of his entrance until he slams the shuttered doors. She turns, startled, to face him.*

Princess   Chance!

Chance   You had some company here.

Princess   Some men were here looking for you. They told me I wasn't welcome in this hotel and this town because I had come here with 'a criminal degenerate', I asked them to get me a driver so I can go.

Chance   I'm your driver. I'm still your driver, Princess.

Princess   You couldn't drive through the Palm Garden.

Chance   I'll be all right in a minute.

Princess   It takes more than a minute, Chance, will you listen to me? Can you listen to me? I listened to you this morning, with understanding and pity, I did, I listened with pity to your story this morning. I felt something in my heart for you which I thought I couldn't feel. I remembered young men who were what you are or what you're hoping to be. I saw them all clearly, all clearly, eyes, voices, smiles, bodies clearly. But their names wouldn't come back to me. I couldn't get their names back without digging into old programs of plays that I starred in at twenty in which they said, 'Madam, the Count's waiting for you,' or – Chance? They almost made it. Oh, oh, Franz! Yes, Franz . . . what? Albertzart. Franz Albertzart, oh God, God, Franz Albertzart . . . I had to fire him. He held me too tight in the waltz scene, his anxious fingers left bruises once so violent, they, they dislocated a disc in my spine, and –

Chance   I'm waiting for you to shut up.

Princess   I saw him in Monte Carlo not too long ago. He was with a woman of seventy, and his eyes looked older than hers. She held him, she led him by an invisible chain through Grand Hotel . . . lobbies and casinos and bars like a blind, dying lap dog; he wasn't much older than you are now. Not long after that he drove his Alfa-Romeo or Ferrari off the Grand Corniche – accidentally? – broke his skull like an eggshell. I wonder what they found in it? Old, despaired-of ambitions, little treacheries, possibly even little attempts at blackmail that didn't quite come off, and whatever traces are left of really great charm and sweetness. Chance, Franz Albertzart is Chance Wayne. Will you please try to face it so we can go on together?

Chance (*pulls away from her*)   Are you through? Have you finished?

Princess   You didn't listen, did you?

Chance (*picking up the phone*)   I didn't have to. I told you that story this morning – I'm not going to drive off nothing and crack my head like an eggshell.

Princess   No, because you can't drive.

Chance   Operator? Long distance.

Princess   You would drive into a palm tree. Franz Albertzart . . .

Chance   Where's your address book, your book of telephone numbers?

Princess   I don't know what you think that you are up to, but it's no good. The only hope for you now is to let me lead you by that invisible loving steel chain through Carltons and Ritzes and Grand Hotels and –

Chance   Don't you know, I'd die first? I would rather die first . . . (*Into phone.*) Operator? This is an urgent person-to-person call from Miss Alexandra Del Lago to Miss Sally Powers in Beverly Hills, California . . .

Princess   Oh, no! . . . Chance!

Chance   Miss Sally Powers, the Hollywood columnist, yes, Sally Powers. Yes, well, get information. I'll wait, I'll wait . . .

Princess   Her number is Coldwater five-nine thousand . . . (*Her hand goes to her mouth – but too late.*)

Chance   In Beverly Hills, California, Coldwater five-nine thousand.

The **Princess** *moves out onto forestage; surrounding areas dim till nothing is clear behind her but the Palm Garden.*

Princess   Why did I give him the number? Well, why not, after all, I'd have to know sooner or later . . . I started to call several times, picked up the phone, put it down again. Well, let him do it for me. Something's happened. I'm breathing freely and deeply as if the panic was over. Maybe it's over. He's doing the dreadful thing for me, asking the answer for me. He doesn't exist for me now except as somebody making this awful call for me, asking the answer for me. The light's on me. He's almost invisible now. What does that mean? Does it mean that I still wasn't ready to be washed up, counted out?

Chance   All right, call Chasen's. Try to reach her at Chasen's.

Princess   Well, one thing's sure. It's only this call I care for. I seem to be standing in light with everything else dimmed out. He's in the dimmed-out background as if he'd never left the obscurity he was born in. I've taken the light again as a crown on my head to which I am suited by something in the cells of my blood and body from the time of my birth. It's mine, I was born to own it, as he was born to make this phone call for me to Sally Powers, dear faithful custodian of my outlived legend. (*Phone rings in distance.*) The legend that I've outlived . . . Monsters don't die early; they hang on long. Awfully long. Their vanity's infinite, almost as infinite as their disgust with themselves . . . (*Phone rings louder: it brings the stage light back up on the hotel bedroom. She turns to* **Chance** *and the play returns to a more realistic level.*) The phone's still ringing.

Chance　They gave me another number . . .

Princess　If she isn't there, give my name and ask them where I can reach her.

Chance　Princess?

Princess　What?

Chance　I have a personal reason for making this phone call.

Princess　I'm quite certain of that.

Chance (*into phone*)　I'm calling for Alexandra Del Lago. She wants to speak to Miss Sally Powers – Oh, is there any number where the Princess could reach her?

Princess　It will be a good sign if they give you a number.

Chance　Oh? – Good, I'll call that number . . . Operator? Try another number for Miss Sally Powers. It's Canyon seven-five thousand . . . Say it's urgent, it's Princess Kosmonopolis . . .

Princess　Alexandra Del Lago.

Chance　Alexandra Del Lago is calling Miss Powers.

Princess (*to herself*)　Oxygen, please, a little . . .

Chance　Is that you, Miss Powers? This is Chance Wayne talking . . . I'm calling for the Princess Kosmonopolis, she wants to speak to you. She'll come to the phone in a minute . . .

Princess　I can't . . . Say I've . . .

Chance (*stretching phone cord*)   This is as far as I can stretch the cord, Princess, you've got to meet it halfway.

Princess *hesitates; then advances to the extended phone.*

Princess (*in a low, strident whisper*)   Sally? Sally? Is it really you, Sally? Yes, it's me, Alexandra. It's what's left of me, Sally. Oh, yes, I was there, but I only stayed a few minutes. Soon as they started laughing in the wrong places, I fled up the aisle and into the street screaming Taxi – and never stopped running till now. No, I've talked to nobody, heard nothing, read nothing . . . just wanted – dark . . . What? You're just being kind.

Chance (*as if to himself*)   Tell her that you've discovered a pair of new stars. Two of them.

Princess   One moment, Sally, I'm – breathless!

Chance (*gripping her arm*)   And lay it on thick. Tell her to break it tomorrow in her column, in all of her columns, and in her radio talks . . . that you've discovered a pair of young people who are the stars of tomorrow!

Princess (*to* **Chance**)   Go into the bathroom. Stick your head under cold water . . . Sally . . . Do you really think so? You're not just being nice, Sally, because of old times – Grown, did you say? My talent? In what way, Sally? More depth? More what, did you say? More power! – well, Sally, God bless you, dear Sally.

Chance   Cut the chatter. Talk about me and *HEAVENLY!*

Princess   No, of course I didn't read the reviews. I told you I flew, I flew. I flew as fast and fast as I could. Oh. Oh? Oh . . . How very sweet of you, Sally. I don't even care if you're not altogether sincere in that statement, Sally. I think you know what the past fifteen years have been like, because I do have the – 'out-crying heart of an – artist'. Excuse me, Sally, I'm crying, and I don't have any Kleenex. Excuse me, Sally, I'm crying . . .

Chance (*hissing behind her*)   Hey. Talk about me! (*She kicks* **Chance**'s *leg.*)

Princess   What's that, Sally? Do you really believe so? Who? For what part? Oh, my God! . . . Oxygen, oxygen, quick!

Chance (*seizing her by the hair and hissing*)   Me! Me! – You bitch!

Princess   Sally? I'm too overwhelmed. Can I call you back later? Sally, I'll call back later . . . (*She drops phone in a daze of rapture.*) My picture has broken box-office records. In New York and LA!

Chance   Call her back, get her on the phone.

Princess   Broken box-office records. The greatest comeback in the history of the industry, that's what she calls it . . .

Chance   You didn't mention me to her.

Princess (*to herself*)   I can't appear, not yet. I'll need a week in a clinic, then a week or ten days at the Morning Star Ranch at Vegas. I'd better get Ackermann down there for a series of shots before I go on to the Coast . . .

Chance (*at phone*)   Come back here, call her again.

Princess   I'll leave the car in New Orleans and go on by plane to, to, to – Tucson. I'd better get Strauss working on publicity for me. I'd better be sure my tracks are covered up well these last few weeks in – hell!

Chance   Here. Here, get her back on this phone.

Princess   Do what?

Chance   Talk about me and talk about Heavenly to her.

Princess   Talk about a beach-boy I picked up for pleasure, distraction from panic? Now? When the nightmare is over? Involve my name, which is Alexandra Del Lago, with the record of a – You've just been using me. Using me. When I needed you downstairs you shouted, 'Get her a wheel chair!' Well, I didn't need a wheel chair, I came up alone, as always. I climbed back alone up the beanstalk to the ogre's country where I live, now, alone. Chance, you've gone past something you couldn't afford to go past; your time, your youth, you've passed it. It's all you had, and you've had it.

Chance   Who in hell's talking! Look. (*He turns her forcibly to the mirror.*) Look in that mirror. What do you see in that mirror?

Princess   I see – Alexandra Del Lago, artist and star! Now it's your turn, you look and what do you see?

Chance   I see – Chance Wayne . . .

Princess   The face of a Franz Albertzart, a face that tomorrow's sun will touch without mercy. Of course, you were crowned with laurel in the beginning, your gold hair was wreathed with laurel, but the gold is thinning and the laurel has withered. Face it – pitiful monster. (*She touches the crown of his head.*) . . . Of course, I know I'm one too. But one with a difference. Do you know what that difference is? No, you don't know. I'll tell you. We are two monsters, but with this difference between us. Out of the passion and torment of my existence I have created a thing that I can unveil, a sculpture, almost heroic, that I can unveil, which is true. But you? You've come back to the town you were born in, to a girl that won't see you because you put such rot in her body she had to be gutted and hung on a butcher's hook, like a chicken dressed for Sunday . . . (*He wheels about to strike at her but his raised fist changes its course and strikes down at his own belly and he bends double with a sick cry.* ~~Palm Garden wind: whisper of 'The Lament'~~.) Yes, and her brother, who was one of my callers, threatens the same thing for you: castration, if you stay here.

Chance   That can't be done to me twice. You did that to me this morning, here on this bed, where I had the honor, where I had the great honor . . .

~~Windy sound rises~~. *They move away from each other, he to the bed, she close to her portable dressing table.*

Princess   Age does the same thing to a woman . . . (*Scrapes pearls and pillboxes off table top into handbag.*) Well . . .

All at once her power is exhausted, her fury gone. Something uncertain appears in her face and voice betraying the fact which she probably suddenly knows, that her future course is not a progression of triumphs. She still maintains a grand air as she snatches up her platinum mink stole

*and tosses it about her; it slides immediately off her shoulders; she doesn't
seem to notice. He picks the stole up for her, puts it about her shoulders.
She grunts disdainfully, her back to him; then resolution falters; she turns
to face him with great, dark eyes that are fearful, lonely, and tender.*

I am going, now, on my way. (*He nods slightly, loosening the
Windsor-knot of his knitted black silk tie. Her eyes stay on him.*) Well,
are you leaving or staying?

Chance   Staying.

Princess   You can't stay here. I'll take you to the next town.

Chance   Thanks but no thank you, Princess.

Princess (*seizing his arm*)   Come on, you've got to leave with
me. My name is connected with you, we checked in here
together. Whatever happens to you, my name will be dragged
in with it.

Chance   Whatever happens to me's already happened.

Princess   What are you trying to prove?

Chance   Something's got to mean something, don't it,
Princess? I mean like your life means nothing, except that you
never could make it, always almost, never quite? Well,
something's still got to mean something.

Princess   I'll send a boy up for my luggage. You'd better
come down with my luggage.

Chance   I'm not part of your luggage.

Princess   What else can you be?

Chance   Nothing . . . but not part of your luggage.

note: in this area it is very important that **Chance**'s *attitude should be
self-recognition but not self-pity – a sort of deathbed dignity and honesty
apparent in it. In both* **Chance** *and the* **Princess**, *we should return
to the huddling together of the lost, but not with sentiment, which is false,
but with whatever is truthful in the moments when people share doom, face
firing squads together. Because the* **Princess** *is really equally doomed.
She can't turn back the clock any more than can* **Chance**, *and the clock*

is equally relentless to them both. For the **Princess***: a little, very temporary, return to, recapture of, the spurious glory. The report from Sally Powers may be and probably is a factually accurate report, but to indicate she is going on to further triumph would be to falsify her future. She makes this instinctive admission to herself when she sits down by* **Chance** *on the bed, facing the audience. Both are faced with castration, and in her heart she knows it. They sit side by side on the bed like two passengers on a train sharing a bench.*

Princess   Chance, we've got to go on.

Chance   Go on to where? I couldn't go past my youth, but I've gone past it.

'The Lament' fades in, continues through the scene to the last curtain.

Princess   You're still young, Chance.

Chance   Princess, the age of some people can only be calculated by the level of – level of – rot in them. And by that measure I'm ancient.

Princess   What am I? – I know, I'm dead, as old Egypt . . . Isn't it funny? We're still sitting here together, side by side in this room, like we were occupying the same bench on a train – going on together . . . Look. That little donkey's marching around and around to draw water out of a well . . . (*She points off at something as if outside a train window.*) Look, a shepherd boy's leading a flock. – What an old country, timeless. – Look –

The sound of a clock ticking is heard, louder and louder.

Chance   No, listen. I didn't know there was a clock in this room.

Princess   I guess there's a clock in every room people live in . . .

Chance   It goes tick-tick, it's quieter than your heartbeat, but it's slow dynamite, a gradual explosion, blasting the world we lived in to burnt-out pieces . . . Time – who could beat it, who could defeat it ever? Maybe some saints and heroes, but not Chance Wayne. I lived on something, that – time?

Princess   Yes, time.

Chance   . . . Gnaws away, like a rat gnaws off its own foot caught in a trap, and then, with its foot gnawed off and the rat set free, couldn't run, couldn't go, bled and died . . .

The clock ticking fades away.

Tom Junior (*offstage left*)   Miss Del Lago . . .

Princess   I think they're calling our – station . . .

Tom Junior (*still offstage*)   Miss Del Lago, I have got a driver for you.

A trooper enters and waits on gallery. With a sort of tired grace, the **Princess** *rises from the bed, one hand lingering on her seat companion's shoulder as she moves a little unsteadily to the door. When she opens it, she is confronted by* **Tom Junior**.

Princess   Come on, Chance, we're going to change trains at this station . . . So, come on, we've got to go on . . . Chance, please . . .

Chance *shakes his head and the* **Princess** *gives up. She weaves out of sight with the trooper down the corridor.* **Tom Junior** *enters from steps, pauses and then gives a low whistle to* **Scotty**, **Bud**, *and third man who enter and stand waiting.* **Tom Junior** *comes down bedroom steps and stands on bottom step.*

Chance (*rising and advancing to the forestage*)   I don't ask for your pity, but just for your understanding – not even that – no. Just for your recognition of me in you, and the enemy, time, in us all.

The curtain closes.

The End.

Notes

page
1   *Hart Crane*: (1899–1932) an American poet and novelist.
2   *Cheryl Crawford*: (1902–86) an American theatre producer
and director who produced Williams's *The Rose Tattoo* in
1951 and later *Sweet Bird of Youth*. Along with Elia Kazan,
Robert Lewis and Anna Sokolow, she is also known for
founding The Actors' Studio, an organisation of theatre
professionals who taught movement and method acting.
Among the famous actors to be trained at the studio were
Marlon Brando, Paul Newman and Geraldine Page.
7   *tabouret*: a small cabinet.
7   *domino*: eyeshade.
7   *Give me the Bromo first*: possibly due to excessive drinking
and drug use, Chance asks for a Bromo-Seltzer, a popular
effervescent antacid.
9   *ether*: an organic compound that was once used as an
anaesthetic.
10   *wire*: telegram.
12   *state line*: border into the next state, out of range.
14   *A pink one*: slang for diamorphine, diacetylmorphine,
acetomorphine.
20   *Palm Beach*: a tropical, beach city in Florida.
20   *I'm the Princess Kosmonopolis*: while there is no direct origin for
Alexandra Del Lago's alias, kosmo/cosmo may refer to the
universe or world and monopolis/monopoly is the exclusive
possession of the trade in some commodity. Her alias, then,
may refer to her sense of grandeur. She ruled the film
universe. Moreover, calling herself 'Princess' resonates with
other references and allusions to children's tales.
20   *Tallahassee*: the capital of Florida and home to Florida
State University. In Southern college towns in the 1950s,
the purchase of alcohol on Sundays was prohibited.

21   *package store*: an off-licence, so called because alcohol had
       to be sold in a sealed container and wrapped up to take
       away.

21   *Old Spanish Trail*: a small highway that spans 3,000 miles of
       the US. This stretch of road, based on an historic trade
       route from the nineteenth century, was completed in
       1929.

23   *neuritis*: a serious nerve disorder, one which results in
       weakness, loss of reflexes and a change in sensitivity.

31   *You wouldn't want 'Confidential' or 'Whisper' or 'Hush-Hush'*: all
       three magazines were popular gossip rags during the time.
       The bi-monthly *Confidential* ran from 1952 to 1978; the
       more blatantly and violently sexual *Whisper* ran from 1946
       to 1958; and *Hush-Hush*, which often ran stories of inter-
       racial affairs and homosexuality, was popular in the 1950s
       and 1960s.

35   *twelve-pound baby*: 5.45 kilos.

35   *the boys belong to the Junior Chamber of Commerce*: JCCs or
       Jaycees are tax-exempt, non-profit organisations for
       youths interested in financial or business networking, like
       the Youth for Tom Finley clubs.

36   *clubs in New Orleans such as Rex and Comus*: while this is a
       reference to social clubs in New Orleans, Rex and Comus
       are a part of Louisiana folk tradition. Rex, the carnival
       king, and his wife visited the court of Comus. This
       meeting of the courts evolved into what today is Mardi
       Gras, the carnival celebrated before Lent.

36   *freshmen at Tulane or LSU or Ole Miss*: first-year students at
       Tulane University in New Orleans, Louisiana, or at
       Louisiana State University in Baton Rouge, or University
       of Mississippi in Oxford, Mississippi.

36   *Oklahoma!*: a popular musical which opened in 1943;
       written and composed by Richard Rodgers and Oscar
       Hammerstein II.

36   *had pictures in 'Life' in a cowboy outfit*: *Life* magazine featured
       articles on political and cultural events. The cowboy outfit
       may refer to his role in *Oklahoma!*.

36   *then that thing in Korea came along*: the Korean War, 25 June
       1950 to 27 July 1953.

37   *swabbies*: enlisted men.

42   *porch*: veranda.

43   *Georgia O'Keefe*: (1887–1986) an American artist, famous
      for her paintings of flowers and desert landscapes.

43   *Pass Christian*: Williams often uses real place names. Pass
      Christian is a costal town in Mississippi.

44   *Discreetly, like you handled that operation you done on my daughter*:
      Dr Scudder performed a hysterectomy on Heavenly. In
      the early- to mid-twentieth century, hysterectomies were
      often performed on women with advanced stages of
      venereal diseases.

46   *There's a pretty fair doctor that lost his license for helping a girl out
      of trouble, and he won't be so goddam finicky about doing this
      absolutely just thing*: the doctor in question has lost his
      licence for performing an abortion, a procedure that was
      illegal in America until 1973. The 'just thing' that Tom
      Junior refers to is castration.

50   *the Queen of Sheba*: in ancient mythology, the Queen of
      Sheba tested King Solomon's wisdom by questioning him.
      She was also known for her gold and gifts.

54   *as if you were buyin' a trousseau to marry the Prince of Monaco*:
      the Prince of Monaco married the American film star
      Grace Kelly, known for roles that exuded innocence and
      sweetness.

54   *backhouse*: an outside toilet.

56   *the black days of Reconstruction*: after the Civil War and the
      emancipation of slaves, the era of Reconstruction
      (1865–77) worked to restructure the power and wealth
      distribution among whites and blacks. Among the
      attempts to reform the South, blacks were given land and
      sometimes money, and some black men were placed in
      government offices. The placing of blacks in government
      offices was, at times, destructive because most had had no
      prior training, let alone a formal education. Before the
      Civil War and the Emancipation, black men and women
      were not even allowed to learn how to read.

58   *novachord*: a polyphonic synthesiser, manufactured by
      Hammond between 1939 and 1942. Only 1069 examples
      were made.

58   *Grant's twelve-year-old?*: whisky.

58   *Walgreen's*: a popular drugstore, much like Boots. In the fifties, Walgreen's would also have had a soda fountain, a counter at which customers could order soft drinks and milkshakes.

59   *He has the length and leanness and luminous pallor of a face that El Greco gave to his saints*: El Greco (1541–1614) was a late Renaissance Spanish painter, sculptor and architect.

61   *outfit Vic Mature wore in a Foreign Legion picture*: although never receiving the attention he deserved from film critics, Victor Mature (1913–99) was one of the busiest and most popular actors after the Second World War. A Southerner like Williams, he was born in Louisville, Kentucky. Mature's popularity waned in the sixties.

61   *Quiereme Mucho*: the song was published in 1931 and became very popular in the thirties. Its English title is 'Yours'.

62   *The Valiant*: a 1920s one-act play by Holworthy Hall and Robert Middlemass, turned into a successful film in 1929. It was nominated for two Oscars and its leading actor, Paul Muni, won an Oscar for his performance. The play is about a convicted murderer who goes to his execution without ever revealing his true identity.

62   *'If you like-a me, like I like-a you, / And we like-a both the same'*: Chance is singing part of 'Under the Bamboo Tree', featured in *Meet Me in Saint Louis* (1944) and sung by Judy Garland.

65   *The Princess Kosmonopolis's best friend is that sob sister, Sally Powers*: sob sister was a derogatory term used to describe female journalists whose reporting style was to evoke sympathy from her readers.

67   *'It's a Big Wonderful World'*: probably the popular Dean Martin song 'It's a Big, Wide Wonderful World'. Its refrain is 'It's swell when you're really in love'.

67   *arpeggio*: a musical term meaning 'broken chord'. The technique requires that instead of playing a chord the notes are played consecutively.

68   *Scarlett O'Hara?*: Chance refers to the infamous Southern belle in Margaret Mitchell's *Gone with the Wind*, an epic

novel that was turned into the famous MGM production, starring Vivien Leigh and Clark Gable, in 1939. When working with MGM, Williams wrote a screenplay about a modern day Scarlett O'Hara, a woman representing 'the natural elegance in the old South' (Williams quoted in Leverich, 509), taking her out of the Civil War period and into the twentieth century. His script, *The Gentleman Caller*, eventually became *The Glass Menagerie*.

70 *There's been a whole lot of Northern agitation all over the country*: Bud refers to movements that condemned segregation and discrimination which continued in America until 1968.

72 *pink pill . . . goof-ball*: slang for diamorphine, diacetylmorphine, acetomorphine.

74 *That's a fine setup, Scotty, if you're satisfied with it but it's starting to give you a little pot and a can*: sitting all day at his job, Scotty is developing a large mid-section and large buttocks.

77 *Lost in the beanstalk country, the ogre's country at the top of the beanstalk*: a reference to Jack and the Beanstalk, the popular fairytale.

80 *Keep your ruttin' voice down*: rutting holds the same vulgar meaning as fucking.

82 *'Bonnie Blue Flag'*: a marching song, also known as 'We are a Band of Brothers', composed in 1861 and associated with the Confederate States of America. For an audience in tune to the racial unrest in America, this march would bring home the extreme racist politics of the Finley clan.

83 *'Liechtensteiner Polka'*: popular folk song composed by the German accordionist Will Glahé.

89 *'a criminal degenerate'*: this phrase was 'usually applied to homosexuals' (Clum, 142). To read Chance as a homosexual is problematic, though. Hence, the phrase takes on the broader meaning of referring to someone who has committed sexual crimes.

89 *You couldn't drive through the Palm Gardens*: Del Lago reveals that Chance is still under the influence of drugs and alcohol.

90 *Grand Corniche*: a winding road along the south coast of France, roughly 2,000 feet above sea-level.

91   *Chasen's*: a luxurious restaurant located in Beverly Hills, California. Chasen's has been a favourite spot for Hollywood stars such as Elizabeth Taylor and Frank Sinatra.

Questions for Further Study

1. Critics insist that the plays of Tennessee Williams, unlike those of his contemporaries such as Arthur Miller, are 'poetic' rather than 'realistic'. What elements of *Sweet Bird of Youth* represent a 'poetic' aesthetic?
2. The protagonist, Tom Wingfield, in *The Glass Menagerie*, says: 'I am the opposite of a stage magician . . . I give you truth in the pleasant disguise of illusion'. How is this an equally accurate description of *Sweet Bird of Youth*?
3. In his 'Foreword' to the play, Williams claimed his use of violence is Aristotelian – that the audience reaches a catharsis (or emotional cleansing) through the watching of violence on stage. To what extent do you see the violence in *Sweet Bird of Youth* offering the audience catharsis?
4. The scholar David Savran argues that while Tennessee Williams has on many occasions spoken out against racism, calling it 'the most horrible thing', he objectifies and exoticises those that are deemed as other within the social setting of his plays, exemplifying 'a contradiction inherent within a certain liberal egalitarianism' (126–7). Assuming this contradiction is apparent in *Sweet Bird of Youth*, which characters are objectified and exoticised, and how so?
5. How does Williams's *Sweet Bird of Youth* fit into the tradition of Southern writing? What comparisons can be drawn between Williams and other Southern writers such as Carson McCullers and William Faulkner?
6. What significance can be drawn from the names of characters (Chance, Heavenly, Stuff, Fly, Boss Finley, etc.)?
7. The action of the play is set '*somewhere on the Gulf Coast*' in the '*Royal Palms Hotel*', in which '*a grove of palm trees*' is ever present on the cyclorama. How does the tranquillity of the luxurious seaside hotel inform the tragedy of the play?

8. A four-lane highway, although never seen on stage, is said to run past the Royal Palms Hotel. What does this image of encroaching modernisation suggest about the time period, place and context of the story, and the relationship between the characters?

9. Taking into account the play's title as well as the '*soft, urgent cries of birds*' and '*the sound of their wings*' that are heard throughout, what is the symbolic significance of 'birds' in *Sweet Bird of Youth*?

10. Throughout *Sweet Bird of Youth*, there are many references to age, ageing and a desire to recapture one's youth. Alexandra Del Lago has fled from the Silver Screen after her close-up reveals her age, and Chance Wayne considers himself old at twenty-nine. What makes youth so sweet and desirable to the characters in this play?

11. From Dr Scudder, the audience learns that Chance's mother has died, and, unable to reach Chance, a collection at her church was taken up in order to bury her. What relevance does the death and burial of Chance's mother have on the play?

12. Del Lago refers to herself and to Chance as 'monsters'. What makes these two characters monstrous? What other characters in the play can be described as 'monsters'?

13. The children's tale of Jack and the Beanstalk is mentioned in Act Two, Scene Two. How does it help to define the characters in this play? How does it inform the plot? What other references to children's fairytales are there and what significance can be attached to them?

14. What is the symbolic significance of Del Lago's need for oxygen and her desire to retire to the moon, a dead planet without oxygen?

15. What is Williams suggesting about Chance and Del Lago's drug and alcohol abuse? How does this form of abuse function in the play?

16. Many of Williams's memorable female characters, such as Amanda Wingfield from *The Glass Menagerie* and Blanche DuBois from *A Streetcar Named Desire*, are described as 'antebellum Southern belles', evoking Scarlett O'Hara in *Gone with the Wind*. In what ways is Miss Lucy part of this

tradition?

17. *Sweet Bird of Youth* may be said to be a play about the tension between needing illusions and being disillusioned. How are the characters of Alexandra Del Lago, Chance Wayne, Heavenly and Boss Finley defined by this tension and how do they cope with it?

18. In Act Two, Scene Two, Chance sings two songs. How does his singing inform the play?

19. Twice we hear of the nude photograph Chance took of Heavenly when she was only fifteen years of age. In the first instance, Chance shows Del Lago the photograph (Act One, Scene Two). In Act Two, Scene One, Boss Finley tells Dr Scudder that the first time he warned Chance to leave town was after he had discovered the photograph of his daughter had been taken. What significance can be drawn from the photograph?

20. How does Boss Finley, a figure of authority and wealth, use his ability to instil values of young masculine power and feminine purity to aid his racist agenda? And why is that agenda crumbling as seen in Miss Lucy's lipstick graffito and the Heckler's ability to shake up Boss Finley?

21. The movie and television industry are both under attack in *Sweet Bird of Youth*. What is Williams's critique of these media? How is his critique of television similar and how is it different to that of his critique of the film industry?

22. *Sweet Bird of Youth* is set in the 1950s and displays the attitudes and politics of the time. Does it still have power and relevance today?

23. Imagine that you are going to direct a production of *Sweet Bird of Youth*. How would you stage a production of the play? What would the set look like? What would the Lamentation sound like? Who would you cast as Chance Wayne and Alexandra Del Lago?

KATHERINE WEISS is an Assistant Professor of English at East Tennessee State University. Her publications include *Samuel Beckett: History, Memory, Archive*, co-edited with Seán Kennedy (Palgrave/Macmillian, 2009), and essays on Sam Shepard and Sophie Treadwell, among other playwrights.

Methuen Drama Student Editions

Jean Anouilh *Antigone* • John Arden *Serjeant Musgrave's Dance*
Alan Ayckbourn *Confusions* • Aphra Behn *The Rover* • Edward Bond
Lear • *Saved* • Bertolt Brecht *The Caucasian Chalk Circle* • *Fear and
Misery in the Third Reich* • *The Good Person of Szechwan* • *Life of Galileo* •
Mother Courage and her Children • *The Resistible Rise of Arturo Ui* • *The
Threepenny Opera* • Anton Chekhov *The Cherry Orchard* • *The Seagull* •
Three Sisters • *Uncle Vanya* • Caryl Churchill *Serious Money* • *Top Girls*
• Shelagh Delaney *A Taste of Honey* • Euripides *Elektra* • *Medea*•
Dario Fo *Accidental Death of an Anarchist* • Michael Frayn *Copenhagen*
•John Galsworthy *Strife* • Nikolai Gogol *The Government Inspector* •
Robert Holman *Across Oka* • Henrik Ibsen *A Doll's House* • *Ghosts*•
Hedda Gabler • Charlotte Keatley *My Mother Said I Never Should* •
Bernard Kops *Dreams of Anne Frank* • Federico García Lorca *Blood
Wedding* • *Doña Rosita the Spinster* (bilingual edition) •*The House of
Bernarda Alba* • (bilingual edition) • *Yerma* (bilingual edition) • David
Mamet *Glengarry Glen Ross* • *Oleanna* • Patrick Marber *Closer* • John
Marston *Malcontent* • Martin McDonagh *The Lieutenant of Inishmore* •
Joe Orton *Loot* • Luigi Pirandello *Six Characters in Search of an Author*
• Mark Ravenhill *Shopping and F***ing* • Willy Russell *Blood Brothers*
• *Educating Rita* • Sophocles *Antigone* • *Oedipus the King* • Wole
Soyinka *Death and the King's Horseman* • Shelagh Stephenson *The
Memory of Water* • August Strindberg *Miss Julie* • J. M. Synge *The
Playboy of the Western World* • Theatre Workshop *Oh What a Lovely
War* Timberlake Wertenbaker *Our Country's Good* • Arnold Wesker
The Merchant • Oscar Wilde *The Importance of Being Earnest* •
Tennessee Williams *A Streetcar Named Desire* • *The Glass Menagerie*